EDUCATION IN COLONIALAND POST-COLONIAL MALABAR: 1920-2006

A SOCIO-ECONOMIC STUDY

EDUCATION IN COLONIAL AND POST-COLONIAL MALABAR: 1920-2006 A SOCIO-ECONOMIC STUDY

Dr K. S. MATHEW
AND
Dr JOSHY MATHEW

GYAN

2016

The Publication of this book has been financially supported by the ICHR and the responsibility for the facts stated or opinions expressed is entirely of the author and do not of the council.

Price : ₹ 305

First Published, 2016

Published by

Gyan Publishing House
5, Ansari Road
Daryaganj, New Delhi-110002
Phone: 9811692060
E-mail: books@gyanbooks.com

Printed at: G. Print Process, Delhi.

Cataloging in Publication Data—DK
Courtesy: D.K. Agencies (P) Ltd. <docinfo@dkagencies.com>

Mathew, Kuzhippalli Skaria, 1939- **author.**
Education in colonial and post-colonial Malabar, 1920-2006 : a socio-economic study / Dr. K.S. Mathew and Dr. Joshy Mathew.
pages cm
Includes bibliographical references.
ISBN 9788121213042

1. Education—Social aspects—India—Malabar—History—20th century. 2. Education—Political aspects—India—Malabar—History—20th century. 3. Education—Social aspects—India—Malabar—History—21st century. 4. Education—Political aspects—India—Malabar—History—21st century. I. Mathew, Joshy, author. II. Title.

LA1154.M35M38 2015 DDC 370.95482 23

Contents

Acknowledgement

This study is the outcome of a research project sponsored by the Indian Council for Social Science Research (ICSSR), New Delhi. We visited many educational institutions, head offices of various organizations, libraries and archives in Kerala for the collection of relevant data throwing light on the theme . We are indebted to Dr. P. A. Fazal Ghafoor, President of the Muslim Educational Society (MES) who shared a lot of information on the education of Muslims in Malabar. The help and support extended by Fr. Paul David, Manager of the Corporate Schools of CSI, Calicut for the materialization of this work are placed on record with deep sense of gratitude. When we visited various educational institutions for acquainting ourselves with their activities, the persons concerned extended their help in various ways. We gratefully remember the interest shown by Sherija Beatrice, Thomas Thekkanat, P.D. Babu, P. E. Shambu Namboodiri, P. A. Parameshwaran, K. Thamban Nair, and K. Sadanandan in this project .

The discussions held in the National Seminar on Education organized by the Institute for Research in Social Science and Humanities (IRISH), at Kannur was a thought-provoking academic exercise where scholars engaged in serious discourses. The presentations made by them were helpful for the analysis of the research problem. We express our sincere gratitude to C. P. Abdul Majeed, the archivist of the Regional Archives, Calicut who took effort to trace some rare documents from archives. We wish to acknowledge our indebtedness to the staff members of the library of the Centre for Development Studies (CDS), Trivandrum, Malabar Christian College, Calicut and IRISH, Kannur for their constant support that made this volume possible.

We are greatly indebted to the Indian Council of Historical Research (ICHR), New Delhi, for the grant released for the publication of this work. We express our heartfelt gratitude to Gyan Publishing House, New Delhi which undertook the publication of this book.

K. S. Mathew
Joshy Mathew

Preface

Education is the basis to the development process of a country. The general perception is that education is a formal and continuous process of learning, by which individuals attain a certain degree of proficiency in diverse branches of human knowledge. The role played by education in the building up of a democratic and secular society and in the promotion of unity and national integration is crucial. People generally consider education as potential force that liberate the society from ignorance, superstition and irrationalities and a driving force of personality development towards a life of peace, harmony and progress. In India, the state of Kerala has secured a unique position in educational development.

In the colonial period Kerala was divided into three territorial units comprising Malabar, Kochi and Travancore. Among these units Malabar was one of the districts of the Madras Presidency and the other two were native states under their rulers. Malabar was generally regarded as economically, socially and educationally backward region. The people of Malabar also did not maintain substantial relation with the people of Kochi and Travancore. The work of social reformers and Christian missionaries were not very active in Malabar as in the case of Kochi and Travancore, on account of which the social and cultural development was not so fast in Malabar. The backward and depressed communities were denied not only education but also their basic human rights like the right to property, use of public roads, and enrollment in educational institutions. But this situation began to change in the second half of twentieth century primarily because of the educational progress in the united Kerala. State achieved great development in education because of the active participation of government and private players.

Our study chiefly focuses on the educational situation in the erstwhile British Malabar region in the colonial and post-colonial period. At the time of the coming of the British, the educational scenario was dominated by traditional methods and upper caste in the society. Only upper caste children, selectively boys were allowed to attain education in the feudalistic society of Malabar. One of the prominent sections of Malabar, the Mappilas were very averse towards secular education and they followed Madrasa education only. The girls' education was also neglected. The initial attitude of the colonial administrators towards the educational development of Malabar was not adequate. Most of the institutions were located in the urban and semi-urban centres and not in the villages and hilly tracts of Malabar.

The active intervention of the government and Christian missionaries in the educational development of Malabar started in the middle of nineteenth century. Through the Wood's Despatch of 1854, the government started the grant-in-aid system to schools managed by the private individuals. Backward and Depressed communities were given special attention in giving education . Special schools, rural schools, rate schools and so on were established for the poor and disadvantaged group in the society. For instance, many Mappila schools were started to liberate the Muslim communities from the parochial religious teachings of the Madrasas. Mappilas were a headache of the British due their recurring revolts since first half of the nineteenth century. Besides, many educational institutions especially for elementary education were established under Local Boards. It was the responsibility of the Local Fund Boards to give financial aid to the primary schools.

At the same time, Protestant Christian missionaries like Basel Evangelical Mission established schools in Kozhikode, Thalassery and many other parts of Malabar which produced significant change in the educational development of this region. It was the Christian missionary organizations who institutionalized education in Kerala. But the hilly regions of Malabar especially Wayanad were neglected by the British in the establishment of educational institutions in the nineteenth century. The number of secondary and higher educational institutions was very low in Malabar when we compare it with Cochin and Travancore. The students of Malabar had to resort to other cities in the Madras Presidency for higher education till the early decades of twentieth century. Moreover, the colonial rulers completely neglected the technical, health and other professional education sectors of Malabar. These areas attained a boost only during the post-independence period.

In the educational development of Kerala the role of private sector was remarkable. Except Christian missionaries, other community organization were very late in the establishment of educational organizations in Malabar. But in the second half of twentieth century community organizations such as MES, NSS and SNDP began to start educational institutions in a small scale neglecting the hilly regions of north Malabar. Various schools and colleges including engineering colleges were established by these community organizations especially in South Malabar. For the construction of buildings and preparation of other infrastructure community members took great pain and they collected maximum fund for the educational institutions.

Agrarian migration of peasant farmers to the high land of Malabar was an important reason for the educational development of Malabar. The peasants who settled for agriculture set up large number of schools in the interior parts of Wayanad, Kozhikkode, Malappuram, Palakkad, Kannur and Kasargode districts of Malabar. Though they started schools primarily for the education of their own children, they were greatly beneficial to the underprivileged and other native sections of the people. They raised money and resources from their poor situation by various means for the beginning of these institutions. Christian communities raised funds in the form of both cash and kind through *Masapirivu, Ulpannapirivu, Pothupani, Pidiyari* and so on. The period from 1939 to 1970 witnessed the establishment of more than 270 educational institutions by migrants in different parts of Malabar.

The study is of great importance to researchers, teachers, educationists and administrators in the county for the study, educational planning and policy formulation on educational development. The unique experience of Kerala especially Malabar is an instance how educational development can be attained in a social and culturally backward region in India. The constant and active effort of the public and private entrepreneurs played a very crucial role in the educational achievement of Malabar. In short, Malabar acquired great progress in primary, secondary, higher and technical education by the end of twentieth century.

Dr. K. S. Mathew

Dr. Joshy Mathew

List of Tables

Abbreviations

BES	-	Bureau of Economics and Statistics
CDS	-	Centre for Development Studies
CKRMTTI	-	C. K. Raghavan Memorial Teacher Training Institute
DDE	-	Deputy Director of Education
DES	-	Department of Economics and Statistics
DTE	-	Department of Teacher Education
ESLC	-	Elementary School Leaving Certificate
HM	-	Head Master
ITI	-	Industrial Training Institutes
JKS	-	Journal of Kerala Studies
JTSLC	-	Junior Technical School Leaving Certificate
KMCT	-	Kunhithuruvai Memorial Charitable Trust
MBTC	-	Mar Beselious Training College
MES	-	Muslim Educational Society
NSS	-	Nair Service Society
PTA	-	Parents and Teachers Association
REC	-	Regional Engineering College
SNDP	-	Sree Narayana Dharma Paripalana Yogam
SSLC	-	Secondary School Leaving Certificate
UTEC	-	University Teacher Education Center

1

Introduction

Kerala has achieved remarkable progress in social development. The world has recognised Kerala's achievements in high literacy, education, life expectancy, low maternal mortality rate and infant mortality rate which are considered chief indicators of social development. It has obtained great progress in all these fields. In the growth of education, the accomplishments of Kerala is incomparable to other states of India. According to 2001 census, Kerala has achieved a high literacy rate of 90.92 per cent as against the all-India literacy rate of 65.38 per cent.[1] In this study we specially analyse the growth of education in Malabar region, which was undeveloped in all spheres of life even after independence.

Malabar, the present northern part of Kerala was a part of erstwhile Madras Presidency of the British in the colonial period. This area continued as a less developed area compared with other parts of Kerala for a long time. The occupations of the people were agriculture in the rural areas, Fishing and trade in coastal areas. The forest areas of the highlands of Malabar were the provenance of pepper, teak and other forests since time immemorial. The entire area consisted of small *Nadus* ruled by kings and it was again divided into *Desams* under *Desavazhies*. The land of Malabar was chiefly owned by landlords belonging to high caste Hindus viz. Brahmins and Nairs; in some places Muslims and Gowdas.

The facilities for education in Malabar were very limited during the colonial period. Till the first half of the twentieth century Malabar had only very few educational institutions. In the villages, small schools known as *Nattezhuthu Pallikkudangal* were established especially in the *Taravads* of prominent Nair and Nambiar families. The teachers of *Nattezhuthu Pallikkudangal* were called *Ezhuthachanmar.* Students from neighbouring *Taravads* and upper caste families were only brought for education in these schools.[2] These sections of people were only allowed to pursue studies in the caste ridden society of Malabar. The students of *Ezhuthupallies* were first taught to write alphabets in sand and later letters and sentences were written on the *Ola* (palm leaf). Literacy was widespread among the Brahmins and Nairs. Sanskrit literature was transmitted to the Nairs by the sixteenth century in Kerala.[3]

Literacy in Sanskrit was confined to upper castes and to a chosen few like astrologers in traditional Kerala. In addition to Sanskrit and Malayalam, Kerala had four other sacred languages in the traditional period, namely Syriac, Arabic, Hebrew and Latin. The main subjects of study were mathematics, literature, Ramayana, Mahabharatha and Bhagavatha.[4] Some children received training in Sanskrit and Ayurveda also.[5] After undergoing their primary education in the *Ezhuthupallies* some children were sent to Kalaries for being trained in Gymnastics and the use of arms. While some other students were sent to study in Sanskrit in vedic schools under well-trained teachers.[6] The children of low caste and bonded agricultural labourers like Pulayas, Cherumars and tribal people of the interior areas of Malabar were out of the purview of education in the arrangements of this type.

Like several other societies in India, education especially higher education was the privilege of the high caste people in Malabar. Higher education was patronised by the rulers and chieftains and it was given to Brahmins only. An example of this patronage was the annual assembly of scholars known as Revathi Pattathanam held under the patronage of the Zamorins of Calicut. A proficiency test in Rigveda conducted in the Katavallur temple (near Kunnamkulam) for Namboothiri students was another important assembly of scholars in Malabar. This competition was called *Katavallur Anyonyam.*[7] Moreover, a Vedic college was founded and endowed richly by Zamorins of Calicut at Tirunavai in Ponnani Taluk for the education of Namboodiri youth. Vedas, Shastras and Hindu mythology were the main subjects of study in these institutions. *Pulayi* in Kurumbranad taluk was another Sanskrit college in Malabar. These colleges were presided over by a Vadhyan or teacher (a scholar in Sanskrit). The test of the students was based on rote memory by reciting and telling verses from the Vedic and other notable texts. Most of the centres of education were for the benefit of the high caste people and general education of the common folk was a neglected area under the monarchy in Malabar.

The immigration of Vedic Brahmins in Malabar increased the importance of Sanskrit language and literature among the people and most of the prominent education centres were dominated by Brahmins. Moreover, Tamil language was also used in Malabar in the thirteenth century A.D. but disappeared after the period of Perumals. But real revolution in the language of Malabar occurred when Thunjanthu Ezhuthachan boldly formulated a Malayalam alphabet sidelining ancient *Vatteluthu* and *Kolezhuthu* in the seventeenth century.[8] Gradually Malayalam became a common language among the people in the indigenous education. Kerala always had an efficient system of village schools where elementary education was imparted.[9] In the indigenous schools boys and girls were permitted and as mentioned earlier *Slogams, Vyagaranam, Sasthrams* and so on were taught.

The educational progress in the princely state Travancore and Cochin was high compared with Malabar. The reason for this steady progress was due to the favourable factors existing in these princely states. Many of the native rulers who were progressive thinkers initiated several measures for educational development in Travancore and Cochin. The opening of commercial plantations, abolition of state monopoly of trade, migration of skilled and un- skilled labourers to the overseas British territories, abolition of slavery and extensive work of missionaries and social reforms among various communities accelerated the speed of modernisation process in Travancore. But the case of Malabar was different because of the political and economic policies followed by the British. The oppressive land tenure system followed by the British created a large number of tenants-at-will and the government strengthened the authority of the landlords. The bulk of the population lived in abject poverty and socio-economic stagnation prevailed in the society.

Table 1.1 : Percentage of Literacy in the Age Group Nine and above 1951

Region	*District*	*Percentage of Literacy*		
		Male	*Female*	*Persons*
	Trivandrum	59	36	47
	Quilon	68	46	57
Travancore	Kottayam	70	52	61
Cochin	Trichur	61	40	51
Malabar	Malabar	41	21	31

Source: P.R. Gopinathan Nair, in *Social Scientist*, 4,8(1976), p. 40.

The above data reveal the educational backwardness of Malabar as against Travancore and Cochin in the first half of the twentieth century.[10] The literacy rate in the southern region of Kerala was higher than that of the Malabar district under

Madras presidency. The educational policy of the British in India was patterned as per recommendations of the Macaulay's Minute of 1935, which envisaged the propagation of western science and literature through the medium of English. The British policy of the promotion of secondary and higher education at the cost of primary and indigenous education completely destroyed the massive base of primary education in Malabar.

The entire age old socio-economic fabric of Malabar underwent a lot of changes during the Mysorean era (1766-1792). Change in the dress of men and women, forbidding polyandry and prohibition of intoxicants were some of the progressive reforms introduced by the Mysorean intruders in Malabar. The feudal setup of Malabar was also affected by this invasion when many of the landlords left their land and escaped to Travancore. In this short period also no measures were initiated by these rulers for the progress of education because they were preoccupied with the collection of revenue from the people and war against the British. The Nair, Mappila and Thiyya peasants and traders of Malabar generally did not pay much attention to the education of their children. The literacy rate of Malabar was low when compare the rate of literacy of Travancore in the post-colonial period also. The average literacy rate of the people of the southern districts of Kerala was 74.42 per cent in 1981 but the same was only 62.60 in the five districts of Malabar in the same period.

One vital relevance of this work is the present debate in Kerala on the role of private investment in the field of education. Education, which mould generations is a matter of intense discussion in Kerala recently due to the difference of opinion between the government and private managements. Through this work we tried to analyse the role of private agencies in education both in the colonial and post-colonial period. We would like to examine the role of direct government intervention by beginning government schools and part played by private management to cater the great need of the common people for education. Another issue we brought under our investigation is the educational backwardness of the Malabar in higher education and gradual progress in collegiate, technical, teacher training and other minor areas of education.

For the present study we have considered the six districts of Malabar viz. Palakkad, Malappuram, Kozhikode, Wayanad, Kannur and Kasargode. The educational institutions under different managements are taken into consideration from each districts. In the general education category, which is the largest in number private aided, government and unaided institutions are specially analysed. Similarly in the study of collegiate education, technical education, teacher training and medical education the same division is adopted. The period of the current study is from 1920 to 2006. The importance of 1920 in the education history of Malabar is the introduction of the Madras Elementary Education Act by the British government. This colonial act provided a new direction to the education system of Madras government. The reason for the ending of this investigation in 2006 is that by this year tremendous changes occurred in the private involvement of education in Kerala. These changes were brought out when the government introduced a new law for the promotion of self-financing education sector.

The educational backwardness of Malabar began to change after independence and formation of unified Kerala in 1956. For the convenience of study the entire work is divided into eight chapters. The first chapter is an introductory chapter which describe the general education condition of Malabar. The second chapter is dedicated specially to the educational system under the British government. As a part of their colonial policies the Madras government introduced several changes in the general education of Malabar district. For the education of Mappila of Malabar special schools were established and grant-in-aid was also provided for the school education in the district. In this area due importance is given to the missionary activities in the progress of education in Malabar. In the case of Malabar, the Basel Evangelical Mission (BEM) was the pioneer of modern education. In higher education also the British made some contribution to Malabar by establishing some colleges.

Third chapter of this work is chiefly designed for the analysis of school education in Malabar after independence. The migration of people from Travancore to Malabar is an important reason for the progress of educational facilities in Malabar. The natives of Malabar, the Mappilas, the Nairs and the Tiyyas made their contributions for the establishment of educational institutions in this part of Kerala. The government started several educational institutions including Lower Primary, Upper Primary and High Schools in Malabar. One important development in the field of education was the beginning of large number of Higher Secondary Schools in Malabar between 1998 and 2001. Besides, with the implementation of Kerala Education Act, 1958 and Kerala Education Rules in 1959 provided a clear direction to the educational improvement of Malabar.

A complete chapter is set apart to trace the progress of higher education in Malabar. A neglected state existed in Malabar when several higher educational institutions were started in Travancore. The Christian migrants, Nair Service Society (NSS), Muslim Educational Society (MES), Sree Narayana Dharmaparipalana (SNDP) yogam and several regional societies, trusts and individuals made great contribution to the beginning of new colleges in Malabar. The government greatly supported this initiative by establishing a university for Malabar region in 1968. At the same time several government colleges were also established in each districts for the educational advancement of the people. A deep examination is made regarding the higher education of Malabar in this chapter.

The sudden growth of schools from primary level to higher secondary level led to the severe scarcity of trained teachers in Malabar. So, the fifth chapter is dedicated to the progress of teacher training institutions in Malabar region. Followed by the Basic Training Schools, in the government and private sector several Teacher Training Institutes (TTIs) were started in different parts of Malabar. The lack of training colleges for B.Ed. course was serious handicap for the High School education in Malabar. This situation underwent a change when universities and private sector started establishing self-financing B.Ed. colleges in Malabar region.

The sixth chapter of our study provides importance for the growth of technical education in the Malabar region. Junior Technical Schools and Industrial Training Institutes were started by the government to give basic industrial training to the students. Very few government engineering colleges existed in the Malabar region. They were not enough for the technical advancement of the work force in this region. After the beginning of very few private aided engineering colleges in Malabar, government sanctioned self-financing engineering colleges in this region and it was a giant leap in the technical empowerment of Malabar area.

The seventh chapter is on the progress of medical, management and law education of Malabar region. For a very long time the Medical College at Kozhikode was the only medical education centre of Malabar. But this situation showed a change with the beginning of Medical Colleges in co-operative and private sector in Malabar. The beginning of Indian Institute of Management (IIM) in Kozhikode was a great step in this field. Besides, several colleges and few university centres and off-campus centres of some universities outside the state have been offering BBA and MBA courses in the Malabar region. The law education in this region received a great impetus with the establishment of a law college in Calicut. All these chapters were followed by a concluding chapter with the major findings of this study. At the end of this work a select bibliography is given with details of primary and secondary sources, personal interviews and souvenirs of various institutions.

References

1. *Census of India, Population Tables-Kerala*, New Delhi, 2001, p. 12.
2. These teachers were usually educated persons from Vatakara, Thalassery and Kuthuparamba to Wayanad. C. K. Narayanan Nair, 'Wayanattile Prachina Vidhyabhyasavum Naveena Vidhyabhyasavum Oru Padanam', in *Rajatha Jubilee Smaranika*, Pulpally, *op.cit.*, p. 31.
3. Kathleen Gough, 'Literacy in Kerala' in Jack Goody (ed.) *Literacy in Traditional Societies,* Cambridge, 1975, p. 134.
4. The children were taught first the letters by practicing them in sand. Then they used *Ola* (palm leaf) and wrote on them using *Ezhuthani* (pen).
5. *Rajatha Jubilee Smaranika*, Pulpally, *op.cit.*, p. 31.
6. A Sreedhara Menon, *Kerala District Gazetteers-Kozhikode*, Trivandrum, 1962, p. 654.
7. A Sreedhara Menon, *A Survey of Kerala History*, Madras, 1996, p. 163.
8. William Logan, *Malabar Manual,* Vol.1, New Delhi, p. 104.

9. K. M. Panikkar, *A History of Kerala 1498-1801*, Annamalinagar, 1960, p. 320.
10. P. R. Gopinathan Nair, 'Education and Socio-economic Change in Kerala 1793-1947' *Social Scientist* 4, 8, (1976) p. 40.

2

Education in Malabar in the Colonial Period

Though there were several indigenous educational institutions the modern education entered the scenario of Malabar with the coming of missionary organisations in the first half of the nineteenth century. In the same period the Madras government under the English East India Company neglected education in Malabar. The early colonial government had no clear and definite educational policy in their territories under administration. Due to this lack of policy either the Governor or the Court of Directors in Madras had no clear direction in the educational development of not only Madras but the whole Madras Presidency. The effects of Macaulay's Minute in 1835 and the beginning of Madras University 1857 began to be felt in the society of Malabar only with the first half of the twentieth century. But the progress of education and resultant increase in the literacy of Malabar are very fast after independence. Like several other parts of the countries the Christian missionaries started educational activities in Malabar also.[1]

Table 2.1 : State of Education in Malabar 1881

Taluks	*Under Instruction*	*Instructed*	*Illiterate*
Chirakkal	9486	17772	275411
Kottayam	5567	12764	147444
Kurumbranad	7944	20206	232874
Wayanad	1370	3853	82868

Calicut	6384	18721	180857
Eranad	5114	14823	276206
Valluvanad	7117	19149	281836
Palghat	11018	25703	305733
Ponnani	12769	27762	352123
Total	**66769**	**160753**	**2105352**

Source: William Logan, *Malabar Manual,* Vol.1, New Delhi, p. 106.

The nature of illiteracy that existed in Malabar can be viewed from the above estimate. The percentage of literacy in Malabar was only 9.75[2]. It was lower than that of Travancore. The British neglected the education of the people of Malabar for several decades though they gained the administrative control of Malabar in 1792.[3] Their involvement in education started only after the second half of the nineteenth century. The estimate of pupils mentioned here came under the control of schools recognised by the Department of Education and the pupil of the indigenous schools are not included in the estimate.

The Structure of General Education in Madras

The loose state of education in Malabar was put under a definite structure only with the introduction of educational rules and regulations in Madras. According to the Madras Educational Rules the educational institutions were divided into two classes-Public and Private.[4] The public institutions were of two classes. The first section comprised institutions under government or local boards or municipal councils known as institutions under public management. The second section included those under the management of private persons or associations known as institutions under private management. Public institutions under private management are divided into aided and unaided. The aided private institutions had received grant from the government treasury.

In the colonial period the schools for general education were broadly classified into two: Elementary Schools and Secondary Schools. In these two sections the elementary schools were common and the largest number of pupil studied in this category of schools. Large majority of the students of Malabar had stopped their studies in the elementary level and they never attended the secondary level. An elementary school contained following standards according to the rules of the government. They were First Standard, Second Standard, Third Standard, Fourth Standard, Fifth Standard, Sixth Standard, Seventh Standard and Eighth Standard. But due to the scarcity of pupil all the above standards were not started in most of the elementary schools.

The aim of the secondary schools by the government was to furnish higher general education to pupil. As per the rules the secondary schools had been sub-divided into Middle Schools and High Schools. The middle school included both Forms and Classes. First Class, Second Class, Third Class, Fourth Class, Fifth Class, First Form, Second Form and Third Form were the classes included in the middle school in the British Period. The High Schools contained the following forms and classes- First Class, Second Class, Third Class, Fourth Class, Fifth Class, First Form, Second Form, Third Form, Fourth Form, Fifth Form and Sixth Form.

1. Lower Elementary- Class I, II, III, IV, V
2. Higher Elementary- I Form, II Form, III Form (E.S.L.C.)
3. High School - IV Form, V Form, VI Form (S.S.L.C.).

The pupils who completed each section successfully were eligible for promotion to the next standard. The successful completion of eighth standard or third form was qualification for the admission of Elementary Teacher Training Schools. After the completion of this training the candidate was eligible for teacher's job in government or recognised elementary schools.

Government's Role in Madras Presidency 1792-1947

The role of the British administration in the educational progress of Malabar was very feeble throughout the nineteenth century. One of the early ways of the British in the education of the Madras Presidency was that the Court of Directors sanctioned a permanent grant of 250 pagodas each for the three schools at Tanjore, Ramanadapuram and Shivaganga in 1787.[5] These school were started by the Rajas of the respective principalities under the instruction of Christian missionaries. Later the missionaries established schools in 1814, 1817 and 1818 in different parts of Madras Presidency and asked for grant from the government.[6] But the Court of Directors having no specific policy of education asked the Madras Government's stand in the issue and this intervention of the Court of Directors forced the government to think actively on the educational situation of the presidency. The Madras administration began to take interest in the private educational institutions in the state.

The British had no information regarding the educational situation of the Madras Presidency though they completed several decades of administration in South India. After the intervention of missionaries in education in Madras they decided to conduct a survey in this field. Sir Thomas Munro ordered an education survey in 1822 and after the survey a report was submitted to the Court of Directors. In the opinion of the government the total number of the indigenous school was about 12,498 and the number of people under instruction was 12,594,193 in the Madras Presidency.[7] On the basis of the report the Court of Director did not take any concrete step for the educational advancement of the Presidency. But Munro took interest in education in the Presidency and proposed two principal schools in each collectorate, one for Hindus and another for Muslims; and later one school in each taluk and to establish around 15 schools in each district. He justified the expenses of this reforms in these words "whatever expense the government may incur in the education of the people, will be amply repaid by the improvement of the country, for the general diffusion of knowledge is inseparably followed by a taste for comforts of life, by exertion to acquire them and by the growing prosperity of the people."[8] But in the implementation stage of the plan of Munro, only three taluk schools were started in each district. Moreover, under his intervention a Committee of Public Instruction and a training school was established in Madras.[9]

The Court of Directors of the Company were not in favour of mass education in the presidency and they believed in the 'downward filtration theory' where the education was given to highest section in the society. In tune with the Bengal Despatch of 1835 the government abolished taluk and collectorate schools in the presidency. It was a severe blow to the mass education in South India. In 1836, the government established a Committee of Native Education and later it became University Board. Madras Governor Lord Elephinstone recommended the beginning of four schools in the presidency viz. Trichinopoly, Masulipattanam, Bellary and Calicut. Finally, to look after the affairs of education in the presidency the government started Council of Education in 1848. Though the Madras government conducted various changes in the organisational structure in the field of education, no significant achievement was made in the development of education.

The Wood's Despatch of 1854 was the turning point in the history of education in India. In tune with the recommendations of Charles Wood the government decided to start new government schools and provide grant-in-aid to private educational institutions not only in India but also in Madras Presidency. The government also decided to start vernacular schools in the interior parts because of the belief that the instruction of the masses could only be conducted in the native language.[10] In Malabar the first Anglo-vernacular school established at Calicut in 1855 and the first grant-in-aid was provided in 1856 to a private Anglo-vernacular school. In the case of grant on half of the expenditure incurred by private schools under head of teacher's salary was reimbursed by the government in the form of grant. The first taluk vernacular school was opened at Malappuram in 1856 and the aim of the school was to give education to the Muslims in Malabar (Mappilas)[11]. In the following year the government established five other taluk vernacular schools in Malabar.

Rate Schools

After the Wood's Despatch of 1854, the responsibility of the Department of Education was taken over by the Director of Public Instruction. The colonial government started a new category of schools in different parts of the Madras Presidency including Malabar in 1864-65. In these new sections of schools, funds required for their functioning were collected from the local people and students in these schools were exempted from fees. The government encouraged the villagers to contribute for the education of their children. The cultivators were subjected themselves to a rate or subscription to maintain school in their villages.[12] In Malabar, the government had established 23 Rate Schools with 1551 children by 1870-71. The community-wise distribution of rate payers and amounts paid by them are the following.

The rate system lost its voluntary aspect and had legalised with the Madras Education Act of 1863. Government started a special collection of rate along with the regular revenue payments by the land holding cultivating classes of the villages. One of the early rate schools in Malabar was established in Palakkad in 1866. Government upgraded this school into a second grade college in 1888.

Table 2.2 : Number of Rate Payers, Pupils and Amount Collected : 1870-71

Classes	*Rate Payers*	*Students*	*Amount (Rs)*
Brahmins	3064	464	5271
Nairs	5500	817	11199
Other Sudras	987	77	1708
Mappilas	1926	29	3251
Total	**11477**	**1387**	**21429**

Source: Report on Public Instruction, Madras Presidency, 1870-71, p.43, Cited in Salim and Nair, *Educational Development....* p. 122.

In Malabar area the Local Boards Act of 1834 helped the establishment of schools. The Madras Elementary Education Act, 1920 is a turning point in the educational history of Malabar. Under section 3(III) of this act, the government constituted District Educational Council in Madras Presidency. The aim of the council was to promote education in each district because the government realised that it was not possible to improve education without the help of local people and resources. The District Education Council of Malabar was constituted in 1921. Grant-in-aid was provided to private schools by the District Education Councils. This council consisted of 31 members including an elected president. The Collector of the District, President of District Board and the Inspector of Schools were the ex-officio members of this council.[13]

Table 2.3 : Members of Malabar District Education Council

Members	*No.*
Ex-Officio Members	3
Elected Members	
District Board	1
Taluk Boards (2 each)	14
Muncipal Councils (1 each)	5
Malabar Mission	1
Roman Catholic Mission	1
Syrian Christians	1
Nominated Members	
Muhammadans	2
Depressed Classes	1
Ladies (Asst. Inspectress)	2
Total	**31**

Source: Home (192) Department of Education, Go. No. 354, 12/03/192, Bundle No.1, Serial No. 31, Regional Archives, Kozhikode.

Missionary Activity in Malabar

Private agencies and individuals made several contributions to the education of the people of Malabar like other parts of Madras Presidency. Christian Missionary societies, both Catholic and Protestant played a vital role in this attempt. The St. Joseph's Boy's School at Calicut was probably the first missionary educational institution in Malabar. It was established in 1793 by Fr. Gabriel Gonsalves under the Diocese of Cranganore.[14] He was a Catholic missionary and this school has become a part of history as it was the first missionary school in Malabar. But in the case of Travancore she had waited till 1817 for the first missionary school.[15] Another matter of importance was that in Travancore, the early schools were started by Protestant missionary societies like CMS and LMS but in Malabar the first institution for education was the contribution of Catholics.

But in the later period the Protestant missionaries took great interest in the spread of the message of Jesus Christ in the countries of Asia and Africa. The members of German Basel Evangelical Mission were the pioneers in missionary activities in Malabar region.[16] At first the decision of the Basel Evangelical Mission Society to work in India was met with some restrictions as the East India Company did not permit non-British missions to work in British occupied territories. The British lifted this restriction with the introduction of the Charter Act of 1833 and permitted non-British missionary societies in British colonies. So three missionaries, John Christopher Lehner, Christian Lenhard Greiner and Samuel Hebich of Basel Evangelical Mission Society were sent to India for missionary activities. They landed in Calicut on 21 August 1834. In Malabar region the Basel Evangelical Mission (BEM) opened the first English school at Kallai in Calicut in 1848.[17]

The Basel Mission's work had spread in several parts of Malabar especially in Tellicherry, Calicut and Palakkad. Their next school was started at Tellicherry in 1856 and it was then known as Basel German Mission School. Nowadays the name of the school has changed as Basel Evangelical Mission Parsi School to mark respect to Kaikose Ruderasha, a Parsi philanthropist who donated money for the development of the school. The third school of this Mission was established at Palakkad known as Basel Evangelical Mission School in 1858. It was started as an English School by a Basel missionary Rev. J. Strobel. To attract more local students it was converted into an Anglo-vernacular School in 1860. Later it was upgraded to Middle School in 1864 and finally it became a High School in 1905.

Native Initiatives in Malabar

Single Teacher Schools

Local school's functioning in Malabar with single teacher was a peculiarity of the education system of Malabar. Schools of this category were normally attached to the Taravads of the houses of the prominent families of that area. Apart from Nair *Taravads* in Malabar the Muslim families of Eranad and Valluvanad taluks started single teacher schools. Many of the schools in the above taluks functioned as a part of the Madrasas in that area.[18] The number of these schools was high in the period between 1950-1960. Only limited number of students studied in these schools and the only teacher taught all subjects up to fourth standard and administered the school in all means. A Government U. P. School started in Kolagappara in 1939 was an example of single teacher school in Wayanad.

One major initiative on the part of the native people to start an educational institution was taken by the Raja of Calicut in 1877. P.K. Manavikrama Raja, the then Zamorin of Calicut started 'Kerala Vidhyasala' in 1877 as per the suggestion of the Malabar collector William Logan for the English education of the members of the family of Zamorin. This is the present Zamorin's Higher Secondary School in Calicut.[19] This school played an important role in the social and political life of the people of Malabar.[20] According to the census of 1881 the following table presents the state of education among the people of Malabar.

Table 2.4 : Progress of School Education in Malabar 1857-58 to 1882-83

	High School	*Middle School*	*Elementary*
Years	*Pupil*	*Pupil*	*Pupil*
1857-58	205	508	116
1862-63	381	577	–
1867-68	753	2012	1013
1872-73	562	3696	11671
1877-78	295	1180	27527
1882-83	431	1431	37196

Source: William Logan, *Malabar Manual,* Vol.-1, New Delhi, p. 106.

Grant-in-Aid System

The colonial government started to issue regular grant-in-aid to the private institutions with the introduction of Wood's Despatch of 1854. The rules and regulations for the distribution of grant-in-aid were very strict and new changes were brought out in 1864-65. In keeping with the amended rules the private schools had to charge fees at a rate fixed by DPI from at least three-fourths of the number of pupils to get grant from the government. The grants would be used for salaries, scholarships, purchase of reference books and furniture, maintenance of buildings and so on.[21] The imposition of fee in the school led to the withdrawal of many students from the school.

The Madras government passed Local Fund Act of 1871 and under this act the responsibility of financing elementary education was accorded to Local Boards.[22] Immediately on the passing of this Act of 1871, the land cess was levied at the maximum rate in the district. When this act came into existence the government abolished education tax and government schools were put under Local Boards. Through this Act funds were provided for the maintenance of elementary schools either wholly or by means of grants-in-aid for the inspection of schools, for the training of teachers and for the construction and repair of school buildings.[23] In fact, through this change the aim of the government was to lesser the financial burden of education in the district and hand over the responsibility of mass education to the heads of local people. In the first of the Act of 1871 the government started five schools under the Boards of Calicut and Tellicherry and two schools under Calicut Municipality.[24]

The scarcity of fund forced the government to gather more funds for the Local Boards by imposing house taxes from the people. The house tax levied under this Act of 1871 was particularly intended to meet the educational expenditure. The imposition of this new tax was strongly opposed to by the people. Consequently the colonial government withdrew the house tax and started providing special grants to Local Boards from the Provincial funds. The government started a new scheme in providing grants to teachers. According to this scheme the grants to teachers were fixed in 1883 at 1/3, 1/4 , 1/5 of the salary, as per the qualifications classified as superior, normal and ordinary despecsively. This system was not beneficial to the private schools because of the non-availability of qualified teachers in Malabar.

Table 2.5 : Government and Aided Schools in Malabar 1858

Type of School	*No. of Schools*	*No. of Students*
Government	7	340
Private by Missionaries	4	403

Source: Data compiled from A. Abdul Salim and P.R. Gopinathan Nair, *Educational Development in India*, New Delhi, 2002, p.121.

In 1886, the government started giving grants to Mappila schools from provincial funds in non-municipal towns and villages. In the early decades of the British period the colonial administrators had paid no attention to educational development of Malabar. But they restored the *Janmi* system and took immediate steps to increase their revenue by raising taxes from the peasants. They especially suppressed the Mappila peasants in connivance with Hindu landlords and it led to the prolonged Mappila uprisings in Malabar (1839-1921). During the time of this insurgency the British took special interest in the Education of Mappilas in Malabar. The authorities find that the lack of secular education among the Mappilas was a reason for the hostile attitude of the Mappilas to the British administration. Several Mappila schools were established in different parts of Malabar especially in Eranad and Valluvanad taluks. Though the government introduced many changes in the education code the achievement in the field of education in Malabar was not significant.

Education of Backward Classes and Women

The British government did not pay much attention to the education of the backward classes and women in the Malabar. Moreover, some of the measures taken by the government in the field of education were not beneficial to the institutions providing education to the pupils of backward classes. The Result Grant system, introduced in Malabar had negatively affected such institutions giving education to the backward communities in Malabar. In the Result Grant system grant was given on the basis of school attendance of the pupils. The authorities were not able to maintain the attendance of the backward section of the society. The grant to these institutions was meagre. This situation forced many school managers to opt to relinquish the government grant.[25]

Unlike the case of Travancore, the government incentive to education was not satisfactory as far as the education of backward communities was concerned. The indifferent attitude of the parents, fear of vaccination, agricultural labour, adjustment problem of backward students in the school and lack of an effective mechanism to bring them to the school were some of the important hindrances of the education of the backward pupils. Government began to take several measures to attract backward children to school from 1885 onwards. Government increased the grant to 50 per cent on the basis of the number of pupils in these communities, but this did not produce desired result. Though the government arranged night and evening schools in Malabar, the government could not attract the backward pupil to the school. The pathetic situation of the education of the backward pupil can be understood from the observation of an Inspector of School in Malabar. "The boys will not attend unless a peon is sent round every morning to fetch them. The teachers had to pay frequent visits to the parents of the pupils and to beg, as a personal favour to themselves that children may be sent to the school."[26] The government could not achieve much progress in the direction of education of women in Malabar.

Tiyyas and English Education

Tiyyas, the prominent community in Malabar, enjoyed the fruits of English education rather than any other native communities in Malabar. In 1844, the British government proclaimed preference in government job to those who had attained English education. Due to the caste consideration the Brahmins and Nairs generally avoided modern education but the Tiyyas of Malabar had no hesitation in acquiring English education.[27] Tiyyas who had education in Sanskrit and English worked as contractors and traders under

Europeans in the major cities of Malabar viz. Kannur, Thalassery, Kozhikode and Palakkad. They utilised the educational facilities in the Basel Missions educational institutions in Malabar because there was no restriction in their institutions on the basis of caste, but at the same time Tiyyas were not permitted in the Zamorins College even in 1918.[28]

Tiyyas who passed Matriculation entered into government service and they even could visit the house of a Brahmin as a part of their official duty. In the beginning of the twentieth century Malabar could see not only clerks in the government service but also Deputy Collectors and Sub-Judges from the Tiyya community. Many tahsildars, lawyers, doctors, principals and journalists of Malabar are from Tiyya community. The educated Tiyya community of Malabar formed in 1906 Sree Jnanodhaya Yogam in Thalassery emulating the path of Ezhavas of Travancore who formed Sree Narayana Dharma Paripalana Yogam in 1903 under Sree Narayana Guru. Like Travancore Sree Narayana Guru led the Tiyyas in establishing many temples in Malabar for Tiyyas.

Education Condition of Mappilas

The Muslim community in Malabar was popularly known as Mappilas. Traditionally they were inland and foreign traders and many of them engaged in agriculture especially tenants under the Hindu Janmies. Their attitude to modern secular education was not satisfactory and Mappila students were mainly engaged in religious education in the Othupallies under Mullas or Musliars. These Othupallies were attached to mosques and the syllabus in these institutions chiefly included skill of reading and writing of Arabic language and the study of Quran. A few students, after the completion of their studies in *Othupallies* had joined in higher classes known as *Dars.*[29] In short, the world of knowledge of Mappilas in Malabar used to end with their education in the *Othupallies* or *Dars*.

In the initial stage of British education in Malabar the Mappilas did not show any interest in it. Besides, they opposed western education. They were unhappy to study any subject other than their Oriental classics and law, literature and theology of Islam. The opposing attitude of the Mappilas towards modern education caused a tension between the British and the Mappilas. The British authorities also realised that the lack of education was an important reason for the recalcitrant approach of the Muslims. So the government took steps to both reorganise the curriculum in the Madrasa education and to open schools in the Mappila-dominated areas. In the all-India level also government adopted several measures on the basis of the recommendations of the Government of India Resolution 1871 and Hunter Commission of 1882 for the encouragement of the education of the Muhammadans in India.[30] In 1917, the number of institutions intended for Mappilas rose from 835 to 867 with an increase of about 3100 students in strength.[31] The government maintained a special training school for Mappila teachers in Malappuram. Very few Mappila students joined other training schools in Malabar district viz., Calicut, Kannur, Thalassery and Palakkad. In the academic year 1920-21 all together 80 Mappila students were trained in Malabar.[32]

The poor educational situation of Mappilas of Malabar was visible from a memorandum of Kerala Provincial Muslim Educational Council sent to the minister of education in Madras. The total Muhammadan male population of the presidency according to the census of 1921 is 14,16,049. In this, the number of Mappilas is 5,43,734. In Malabar and South Canara district there were four second Grade College and two first grade colleges.[33] The demand of the Mappilas for separate assistance for education of their community was rejected by the government and the memorandum did not yield any result.[34]

The government had introduced arrangements to teach Malayalam and arithmetic in the Othupallis with the help of Mullas. A special training was provided to the Mullas in teaching Malayalam to the children of the elementary schools and government conferred salaries and grants on the basis of number of children attending schools of that kind. When the Mappila students expressed reluctance to attend the schools opened for Hindus, the government started special schools named Mappila Primary Schools in Malabar. But the earnest effort of the government for the improvement of the education of the Muslims did not yield desired result. The number Mappila students was very low in the schools of Malabar though the government took several measures for their education. One dreadful feature of this period from 1868 to 1871 was that not a single Mappila girl child attended the educational institutions of Malabar. But at the same time 1546 Hindu girls attended the schools. The table below shows the picture of the progress of Mappila education in Malabar.

Table 2.6 : Number of Boys Attended in the Schools in Malabar 1868 to 1871

Year	*Europeans*	*East Indians*	*Native Christians*	*Hindus*	*Mappilas*	*Total*
1868-69	36	601	1589	9649	309	12184
1869-70	5	709	1870	11412	348	14354
1870-71	**23**	**575**	**1898**	**11439**	**369**	**14324**

U. Muhammad, *Educational Empowerment of Kerala Muslims: A Socio-Historical Perspective*, Calicut, 200, p. 24.

Educational Initiatives among Muslims

In the early decades of the twentieth century, Muslims showed some signs of renaissance in Malabar. Some of the progressive leaders expressed their interest in the spread of modern secular education in the community. Kunju Muhammad Haji Manappad, Seethi Muhammad Haji Kottapurath, K. M. Seethi Sahib, K. M. Moulavi and Vakkom Moulavi formed *Ayikka Sangam* in 1922. *Ayikka Sangam* provided scholarship to students for the promotion of education.[35] Though it was formed in Kodungaloor (Kochi) it could inspire many Muslim students to modern education in Malabar. Through the activities of *Ayikka Sangam* in Thalassery many students were attracted to higher education in Malabar. The opposition of conservative Muslim community was a vital cause for the end of *Ayikka Sangam* in 1938. Kerala Muslim Educational Association (KMEA) was formed in 1950 in Ernakulam for the educational promotion of Muslim students. B. Pokkar Sahib and K. M. Seethi Sahib founded KMEA. Its chief activity was providing scholarship to students. In 1956, KMEA provided Rs 8000 to Muslim students in the form of education scholarship.

Raja's Schools in Malabar

Like the Zamorin's of Kozhikode local chieftains established schools mainly for the education of the children of royal families. Most of the Raja's of Malabar started their own schools in Kerala. Rajas's High School, Chirakkal, Rajas's High School, Kollengode, Kadthanad Raja's High School, Purameri, Rajas's High School, Kottakal and Rajas's High School, Neeleshwaram came under this category.

Schools for General Education

The schools of modern line were started with the establishment of British administration in Malabar. But the children had to travel by walk up to five miles to reach a lower elementary school and 15 miles to reach a higher elementary school.[36] When Madras Local Board Act was passed in 1834 *Taluk* Boards, District Boards and Municipalities were established and they took the responsibility of education in the districts.[37] District Education Councils were set up and they provided grant to private educational agencies. Several of them were managed by single teachers. The trained teachers in Elementary School for boys got Rs 12 and school for girls get Rs 13.[38]

Before independence the Christian migrants of Malabar established several schools in the hill tracts of Malabar. One of the earliest schools started by migrants in Kozhikode was St. Mary's Lower Elementary School at Maruthomkara in 1937.[39] It was first started in shed made for the purpose of church.[40] This school offered was a great opportunity for the students of many neighbouring areas. The migrants of Rajapuram in Kasargode established a school in their colony of migration in 1943, the same year of their settlement.[41] This school got recognition in 1945 and came to be known as Holy Family Lower Elementary School. This school had trained teachers as some of the migrants in this colony were teachers.

Higher Education

The contribution of the colonial government was not impressive. Before independence the British government established only three colleges in Malabar. This included both first grade and second grade colleges. Victoria College Palghat, Brennen College, Thalassery and Malabar Christian College (MCC), Calicut were the colleges in Malabar. The MCC was the only private management college in the colonial period and it was managed by the Basal Evangelical Mission. The Municipal Council of Thalassery sanctioned a subsidy of Rs 7936 to Brennen College Thalassery in 1921.[42] The Brennen College under Municipal management was taken under government management in 1920. The Victoria College was taken over by the government from Palghat Municipality in 1920.[43]

In the colonial period both the private agencies and the government played their own role for the education of Malabar. By providing grant-in-aid the government encouraged the private participation in education. The schools, established by the Christian missionaries aided the education of backward sections and women in the society. The activities of the government in this field did not yield desired result in this matter. Besides, the government tried to promote education among the Mappilas and Thiyyas in the society in Malabar.

References

1. William Logan, Manual Vol. 1, New Delhi, p. 106.
2. The total population of Malabar in 1881 was 2,332,874.
3. In the Third Anglo-Mysore war (Refer to the Author) the defeated Tipu Sultan ceded Malabar to the British through the Treaty of Srirangapattanam in 1792.
4. *Madras Educational Rules 1941*, Government Press, Madras, 1941, p.1.
5. P. N. Chopra, T.K. Ravindran, N. Subramanian, *History of South India*, New Delhi, 2003, p.183.
6. For more details see *Ibid*, p.184.
7. *Ibid*, p.184.
8. *Op. cit*, p.185.
9. This was the first teacher training institution in South India. Each district can send two candidates to this school for training, one Hindu and one Muslim for training and they were given a stipend of Rs 15 per month. For more information P. N. Chopra *et.al.*, *op. cit*, p.185.
10. A. Abdul Salim and P.R. Gopinathan Nair, *Educational Development in India*, New Delhi, 2002, p.121.
11. *Op. cit*, p.121.
12. J. Mangamma, *The Rate Schools of Godavari*, Hyderabad, 1973, p.1.
13. *Home (192) Department of Education, Go. No. 354, 12/03/1921,*

Bundle No. 1, Serial No. 31, Kozhikode Regional Archieves. (Hereafter KRA)

13. *Home (192) Department of Education, Go. No. 354, 12/03/1921,* Bundle No. 1, Serial No. 31, Kozhikode Regional Archieeeves. (Hereafter KRA)
14. Later in 1892 Monsignor Michael Antony set up the St. Joseph's Girl's High School in Calicut. He was the Bishop of Mangalore. For more details of missionary activities in the field of education. For more details of missionary activities in field of education see Geo Payyapilly, *Prakasharekha*, Calicut, 2005, pp. 222-223.
15. The first school in Travancore was established in 1817 by a Church Mission Society missionary Rev. Thomas Norton at Alleppey.
16. The German Missionary Society became Basel Evangelical Mission Society on 25th Sep. 1815 at Switzerland. The aim of the BEMS was the spread of the Good News.
17. This school later became the famous Malabar Christian College in Calicut in 1909.
18. Information given by K. K. Naha, Parappanagadi. He was a member of the Kizhakkiniyath Taravad, where a single teacher school functioned. Originally it was started as a part of a Madrasa.
19. The origin of the famous Zamorin's Guruvayurappan College also was from this humble beginning of this school in 1877.
20. Several great luminaries of the modern Kerala history were the alumni of this school. K. P. Kesava Menon, S.K. Pottakkad, V. K. Krishna Menon, P. P. Ummar Koya, C. H. Muhammad Koya and so on were the old student of this school. The first student's strike of Malabar occurred in Zamorin's School in 1902 known as 'Shirt Strike'. The strike was to get permission to wear shirt without tie. Information given by P. K. Sree Manavedan Raja, Zamorin of Calicut, 2009.
21. Salim and Nair, *op. cit.,* p.122.
22. The Madras Local Board Act of 1871 repealed the District Road Cess Act III of 1866 and the Education Act of VI of 1863.
23. Mangamma, *op. cit,* p. 57.
24. Salim and Nair, *ibid,* p. 124.
25. Salim and Nair, *op. cit.,* pp.122-23.
26. Report of Public Instruction, Madras Presidency 1970-71, p. 42. Cited in Salim and Nair, *op. cit.,* p.127.
27. K. K. N. Kurup, *Adhunika Keralam: Charitra Gaveshana Prabhandagal,* Thiruvanathapuram, 1995, p. 21.

28. But at the same time Madras University's text book in Malayalam second language for Intermediate course 'Jahnara' was written by Murkoth Kumaran, a Tiyya from Malabar *Ibid.,* p. 26.
29. Ponnani Dar constructed by Shaikh Fariduddin was a famous Dar of Kerala. Ponnani has been an acclaimed religious education centre of Muslims in Kerala.
30. For more details refer U Muhammad, *Educational Empowerment of Kerala Muslims-A Socio-Historical Perspective,* Calicut, 2004, p. 24.
31. *Report on Public Instruction in Madras Presidency 1917-18,* Vol. 1, Madras, 1919, p. 11.
32. Law (1922), *Department of Education,Ordinary Series Go. No.497, 20/04/1922,* Bundle No. 1, Serial No. 78, (KRA).
33. Law (1926). *Department of Education,Ordinary Series Go. No.1987, 20/10/1926,* Bundle No. 4, Serial No. 67, (KRA).
34. The taluks in Malabar having large Mappila population are Eranad, Walluvanad, Ponnani and Calicut. There were secondary schools for boys in these taluks. Two schools which are under private management are specially for Mappilas. One of the important reason for the opening of separate schools for Muhammadans is that their vernacular (Urdu) was different from the vernacular of the other communities. This difficulty does not arise in the case of Mappilas whose vernacular is same as that of other communities of Malabar viz. Malayalam. Adequate facilities for secondary education exist in Malabar. The number of secondary school was 49 and Mappilas can partake of these in common with other classes and communities. Government sanctioned financial assistance in 1924 to YMCA in connection with their activities for the improvement of the economic condition of Mappilas. They established a small industrial school for Mappilas at Areekode. Instruction imparted has been confined to weaving, cane work, carpentry and sericulture. Explanation from the government regarding the memorandum of the Kerala Provincial Muslim Educational Council. Law (1926) *Department of Education,Ordinary Series Go. No.1987, 20/10/1926,* Bundle No. 4, Serial No. 67, (KRA).
35. The rate of scholarship was five rupees for High School students, Rs 10 for college students and Rs 15 for students of medicine and engineering in Aligarh and Madras. For additional information *MES Charithram 1964-94*, Calicut, 1994, p. 22.
36. *Girideepam, Special issue, op.cit.*, p.19.

37. Malabar Local Board was started in 1859 with the objective of promoting primary education in the rural areas. Later Elementary Education Act was passed in 1920 to establish elementary schools.
38. *Report on Public Instruction in Madras Presidency 1919-20*, Vol. 1, Madras, 1921, p. 2.
39. The date of the inauguration of the school was 01-03-1937.
40. When this shed was destroyed in fire it was shifted to Mullamkunnu where Joseph Iyyalil and Mathai Kizhakkayil donated land for church and school. For more details on the growth of this church see *Edavaka Directory 2008*, St. Mary's Forane church, Maruthomkara, 2008, pp. 55-56.
41. The migration of Knanaya Christian farmers from different parts of Kottayam (Punnathara, Kattachira, Kidangur, Mattakara, Kudallur, Piravam, Arunoottimangalam, Chengalam, Karinkunnam, Chungam and Muttam) to the northern parts of Malabar is a best example of organised migration. When the Syrian Christians scaled successful migration to Malabar the Bishop of the Diocese of Kottayam encouraged Knanaya Christians to migrate to Malabar. He entrusted V. J. Joseph (Professor, St. Aloysius College, Managalore and President, Knanaya Catholic Congress) to make arrangements for the settlement of people in Malabar. He purchased 1800 acres of Janmam land in Eachikol in the Panathadi village of Hosdurg Taluk in the then South Canara district in 1942 for the settlement of farmers from Kottayam.The Bishop sent 72 families to this land and distributed land to them. This settlement location was given a new name called Rajapuram and later came to be known as 'Rajapuram Colony'. Alexnagar and Ranipuram were the two such other colonies of migration in Kasargode. For more information see *Malabar Knanaya Suvarna Jubilee Smaranika 1943-1999*, Kannur, 1993, pp. 10-13.
42. Municipal Council consist of Chairman, Vice-Chairman and 14 members. *Home (1922) Department of Education, Go. No. 326, 13/03/1922,* Bundle No. 1, Serial No. 25, Regional Archives, Kozhikode.
43. *Report on Public Instruction in Madras Presidency 1919-20*, Vol. 1, Madras, 1921, p. 1.

3
General Education: 1947-2006

Malabar, after independence was not included in the state of Kerala, but continued till 1956 as a district under Madras state. The district did not receive much attention during the ten years under Madras state. The combined effort of both the government and private agencies caused progress in the education situation of Malabar. At first the interest for education was taken by the newly settled migrants in the highland of Malabar. The migrants included Syrian Christian, Ezhava, Nair, Muslim and few backward sections of Travancore. The migrants from Travancore attached great importance to the education of their children in Malabar. A drastic change in the education of Malabar was witnessed with the large scale migration of people from Travancore to Malabar. The successive governments of Kerala sanctioned several new schools in government sector and upgraded board schools and early government schools in the colonial period. In this chapter an analysis of the role of private sector and government's initiative in the educational development of Malabar has been made.

The literacy rate of Malabar was low compared with Travancore and Kochi at the time of independence. The three districts of Malabar viz. Palghat, Kozhikode and Kannur were below in the percentage of literacy rate in comparison to any other districts of Kerala according to the first census after independence. In all three taluks of Malabar the percentage of total literates of Malabar was below the state average of 40.54.

Table 3.1 : Percentage of Literate Population by Districts in Kerala 1951

Districts	*Male Literates*	*Female Literates*	*Total Literates*
Trivandrum	51.02	31.39	41.15
Quilon	53.58	35.77	44.70
Alleppey	61.85	44.04	52.87
Kottayam	59.69	46.27	53.08
Ernakulam	54.52	36.38	45.43
Trichur	50.11	33.11	41.19
Palghat	33.95	20.76	27.08
Kozhikode	41.14	17.31	29.13
Cannanore	46.47	27.37	36.14
Total	**49.83**	**31.51**	**40.54**

Source: Statistical Outline of Kerala, Dept. of Statistics, Govt. of Kerala, Trivandrum, 1960, p. 61.

Changes in School Pattern

From 1956-57 to 1958-59 the primary section consisted of Standards I to VIII. From 1959-60 onwards it comprised Standards I to VII. While from 1956-57 to 1958-59 secondary section had standards IX to XI. During 1959-60 standard VIII to XI were in the secondary section. Standards VIII to X were in the secondary stage from 1960-61 onwards.

Schools of Private Management

Education and social mobility are closely related. Most of the social reformers in India realised the role of education in the social upliftment of their community. Here the term social mobility simply means an individual's opportunities for social progression. A well educated person can move from one social stratum to another very easily. It is called vertical social mobility. Even disadvantaged classes could ascend the social ladder through education and even the entire family background of an individual will change when he acquire a good job in the society. In the social mobility people became more advantageous social class and in future his family gets higher chances of embarking a long educational career and gaining higher level qualification than those from less advantaged classes.[1] Lack of this educational opportunity was serious problem of Malabar for a very long time. This handicap of Malabar region in education began to be overcome with the wide spread participation of private agencies in the beginning and running of educational institutions. The Christian migrants from Travancore, Nair Service Society (NSS), Muslim Educational Society (MES), Sree Narayana Dharma Paripalana (SNDP) Yogam and a number progressive individuals and several cooperative societies and trusts involved themselves in the educational development of Malabar.

The migrants were well connected with literacy in their native state. The bulk printing in Central Travancore produced daily newspapers and weekly journals. It has made possible a number of social structural changes that would otherwise have been difficult or impossible.[2] Many of the migrants left their children to their relatives in Travancore to continue their education when they moved to Malabar in search of land. They had to find out new facilities for their children because most of them discontinued their studies in Travancore to migrate to Malabar. In the highlands of Malabar they had very little facility to educate their children. The few elementary schools run by the government in one or two places of a taluk were not enough for educational needs of the large scale migrants. Consequently, within one or two years the migrant farmers constructed schools and appointed teachers in most of the colonies of migration.

In many newly originated areas of migration the migrants resorted to schools called *Kudipallikudams* for the education of their children. In such schools one teacher (*Ashan*) used to teach the students alphabets and numbers and basic calculations. The teaching in *Kudipallikudams* was called *Nilatheyuthu* and teachers were called *Nilatheyuthu Ashanmar*. In such schools students had to study by writing in sand specially spread in the floor. In Kottiyur, K.K. Gopalan Nair started a *Kudipallikudam* in the land of Mathai Munjanattu in 1954. In some areas makeshift buildings erected as churches were also used as Kudipallikudams. In Kunnoth such a school functioned in the church building and Devasia Pazhayamballil worked as single teacher up to fourth standard.[3] The parents of the children contributed an amount every month for the salary of the teachers. These teachers were not trained but had received basic education from Travancore.

The migrants had given top priority to the education of their children immediately after their settlement. For the construction of schools the migrants donated land, money and materials generously. Earlier small sheds were made in the land both for worship and education. Sometimes they used the church as school. In most of the places like Payyampally, Thariyode, Nadavayal and Mullankolly, schools were built along with the churches. All the school buildings constructed in the areas of migration were entirely with the money raised from the migrants. Even in the face of harsh living conditions and struggle for survival they found their own ways and means of imparting formal and informal education to the children.[4] For the construction of various buildings including schools and churches under the initiative of the migrants fund was raised through *Azhchapirivu* (weekly collection), *Masapirivu* (monthly collection), *Ulppannapirivu* (collection of products) and *Pothupani* (voluntary labour) by the people of each parish. *Masakkuttam* was another device for raising money for the construction of schools. In *Masakuttam* 15 to 20 families under a parish used to meet every month and collect rupees one or two from each family every month. After one or two years the entire amount was contributed to a public purpose in the parish including the construction of the school.

They started church and school at the same time. In many cases the building for the church functioned as schools. In Sundays religious ceremonies were held in these buildings. Early schools, were small sheds made of bamboo and thatched with grass. One of the chief problems faced by children of the migrants was malaria and common fever. Due to this problem the children were not able to attend the class regularly. The attendance in the schools was reduced to five or six from the original number of 30 to 35 children due to malaria and other diseases.[5] Sometimes the school children fell down exhausted in the school due to fever. The teachers had to take them to their respective houses.[6] The educational officials of the Madras government who visited the schools for inspection were not ready to enter into the classrooms where the students were shivering and fell unconscious due to fever. The officials even ensured not to drink even a drop of water from the schools fearing the attack of fever.[7]

The lack of teachers with enough training was another important challenge to the early educational sector in the areas of migration. In most of the cases people among the migrants who completed fourth standard, taught students in the schools of migration centres. These schools were single teacher schools and he had to manage two or three standards singly. Later the migrants brought trained teachers from Thrissur, Pavaratty, Enammavu and Menachil areas of Travancore and Cochin[8]. These teachers had to work on very low remuneration or even without remuneration. In some schools the teachers were paid their wages in kind like food items. Besides, the teachers who underwent training in the native state of Travancore felt it very difficult to get their degrees recognised in Malabar state under Madras presidency. So even after many years of independence the education milieu of Malabar was in a poor condition. The following table exhibits the relative backwardness of education in the Malabar region. When the migrants established large number of schools in different parts of Malabar, the scarcity of teachers was very severe. In some places this handicap was overcome by appointing nuns from different congregations temporarily.[9]

After the small beginning of the schools by the migrants its full growth as a school of modern line was guided by the parish priests of the churches of a particular area. A 'School Committee' under the parish priest was formed to deal with the government authorities to get the necessary official sanctions for the school. During that time the approval of the government was essential for starting a new class. The ordinary farmers had no knowledge of official formalities and English language used in the government offices. So the help of priests was a great thing to the migrants. The visit of the Deputy Inspector of Education was a nightmare to the teachers and manager of the schools at that time.[10] At the time of the visit the lack of the required number of students would result in the loss of the division and thereby the job of the teacher. Moreover, the annual increment of the teachers would be withdrawn if the students did not answer the questions asked by the Deputy Inspector of Education.[11]

Lack of Teachers and Educational Qualification of Teachers

There were no trained teachers in the nearby areas when St. Joseph L. E. School was established at Kunnoth, hence teachers were brought from other schools in Kuttuparanmba.[12] In many areas the teachers were brought from Travancore after earnest exertion of several months.

Qualified Catholic nuns were brought from Travancore when a school was started in Kudiyanmala. Later a convent of Franciscan Clarist Congregation was started for these nuns.[13] The lack of teachers was serious handicap of the new school started at Pariyapuram by the migrants, which the farmers were not able to solve.[14] The parish priest brought six nuns of Bethany Congregation from West Hill in Calicut as the teachers of this school. They were qualified and four of them were appointed as new teachers of this school and Sr. Seelia became the Head Mistress of this school.[15] The priests forced the teachers to stay in Malabar for the education of the children when they desired to return to their native places.[16]

The education of Tiru-Kochi consisted of first four standard and a 'Preparatory' class of one year before entering first standard. After the completion of 11 years of school education one can go for the Teacher Training Course (T. T. C.) of one year and those trained in such institutions were chiefly appointed in the schools in Malabar. But the students of Malabar joined to the T. T. C. of two years after the completion of eighth standard of school education. But the salary of the teachers in Malabar who were trained in Malabar was higher than those trained in Thiru-Kochi.[17]

Education in Kozhikode, Malappuram and Palakkad

The urban areas of Kozhikode and Palakkad had some prominent higher educational institutions during the colonial period itself.[18] But the general education scenario of the rural areas of these districts was completely dismal. Later by 1940's large number of schools were established in these places especially after the settlement of migrants. The chief centres of migration in the modern Kozhikode districts are Kuttiyady, Maruthomkara, Kulathuvayal, Vilangad, Koorachundu, Kodencherry, Thiruvambady, Koodaranji and Thottumukkam. Nilambur, Edavanna, Karuvarakundu, Mariyapuram, Chungathara, Edakkara, Manimooli, Adakkakundu and Vazhikkadavu were the migration centres of Malappuram district. The district of Palakkad also had some centres of migration like Mannarkkad, Pottassery, Palakkayam, Irumbakachola and Poonchola.

The elementary school started at Maruthomkara in 1937 became a Higher Elementary School in 1951. It was due to the effort of the school committee under parish priest Joseph Kizhakkebhagam. But the long cherished dream of the poor farmers was to start a High School for the students who completed their studies in Higher Elementary School. The students had to go either Kulathuvayal or Vattoli for their high school education and only very few continued their studies by reaching these schools. In this circumstances the concerted effort of the migrants resulted in the upgradation of the school to a High School in 1957.[19] The new High School provided higher education facility for the students from the Primary Schools of Kunduthode, Chembanoda, Chanthankottunada, Padathukadavu, Devarkovil and Chappanthottam. The buildings constructed for the schools were fully funded by the migrants. The beginning of a High School was a great relief to the students because they had to travel 20 kms. to distant Government High School at Perambra.

The establishment of a High School in 1954 at Kulathuvayal was another important event in the educational history of Kozhikode. Earlier it was the St. George Higher Elementary School which functioned in a few sheds. Due to the eagerness of the migrants to get a High School in 1952 itself the migrants constructed a permanent building for it. During that time the school authorities had to get permission from the department of education of Madras to start a new High School in Malabar. Under the inspiration of His Excellency A. M. Patroni, the then Bishop of Calicut Diocese, the parish priest of Kulathuvayal church Fr. C. J. Varkey took initiative to start a High School. Before that the migrants applied for the school but it was rejected by the government[20].

Fr. C. J. Varkey had to stay 10 days in Madras to get sanction for the school. The security amount to be paid to the government for High school, Rs. 5000, was given by Bp. Sebastian Vallopally. The Members of the Legislative Council also helped him in Madras for the school.

In Padathukadavu, without the permission of the government the migrants started a school for the children who discontinued their studies in Travancore. In 1947, a small shed was built near the Holy Family church for the purpose of school. Cyric Mahapilla Mappilakunnel was the only teacher for three classes. He taught all subjects to the children. In 1948, this small education centre received recognition from the government under Fr. Joseph Chungath. The name of this new school at Padathukadavu was Holy Family Lower Elementary School. In the first year itself this school had all together one hundred students in four divisions[21].

In Kodenchery also migrants organised a school near a room attached to the shed of the church in 1946. It was a single teacher school under a migrant called Tommy Thoppil. Besides, very small educational institutions known as *Kalaries* functioned under the teachers known as *Ashanmar*. Under Fr. Fabiyus (1949-1952) this one teacher school became St. Thomas Lower Elementary School in 1950. The need of the migrants was a High School in Kodenchery and it was achieved by the migrants with the effective leadership of Fr. Dosithevus (1952-1959) in the year 1954.[22] This school became a Higher Secondary School in 2000.

The migrants of Koodaranji with the help of Fr. Bernadin started St. Sebastian's school in 1949 and immediately it was recognised by the education department in Madras as St. Sebastian's Lower Elementary school. According to the school register in the first year 138 students were admitted in four classes. In the next year itself it became Higher Elementary School. Due to the effort of the common people in 1962 this institution became a High School and finally in 1998 it became St. Sebastian's Higher Secondary School.

Vilangad, one of the steep hilly regions of migration in Kozhikode district a school was established in 1956 under Fr. Alex Manakkatumattam. Before that several *Kalari* form of educational institutions stared in Vilangad. This school began functioning with government recognition in 1957 under the name St. George L. P. School, Vilangad. The effort of the migrants resulted to the up- gradation of this L. P. School into a U. P. school in 1964. Later in 1968 this U. P. school became a High School and it was the only High School of that area for the people.[23]

Table 3.2 : The Schools Started by Migrants in Malabar before the Formation of Kerala State

	Name of School	*Name of Priest*	*Place*	*Year*
1	St. Mary's L. E. School	Ziarose S. J.	Maruthomkara	1937
2	Holy Family L. E. School Rajapuram	Rajapuram Kattapurath Priesi	Fr. Lukka	1945
3	St. Joseph L. E. School	Fr. Joseph Kuttor	Kunnoth	1946
4	Holy Family L. E. School	Joseph Chungath	Padathukadavu	1948
5	St. Sebastian's L. E. School	Bernadin C. M. I.	Koodaranji	1949
6	St. Thomas L. E. School	Fabiyus C.M. I.	Kodenchery	1950
7	St. Joseph's Aided U. P. School	Joseph Kuthoor	Chempanoda	1953
8	St. George L. P. School	Alex Manak-atumattam	Vilangad	1956

Source: Complied from various souvenirs of Christian churches in Malabar by the author.

The education facilities of Malappuram were not sufficient to population at the time of independence. The Muslims who constituted majority of the population had to wait a couple decades for educational advancement in this district. This district was formed on 16 June 1969, earlier this area was divided in Kozhikode and Palghat districts. The educational backwardness of the hilly areas of Malappuram was addressed by the migrants and the diocese of Bathery. Under the initiative of the diocese a school started in 1982 in Erumamunda with 98 students. The Nirmala High School became a higher Secondary School in 1998 as a leading institution in Malappuram.[24]

St. Mary's High School at Pariyapuram is a notable educational institution under the Diocese of Thamarassery in Malappuram district. The migrants of Pariyapuram built a Lower Primary School in 1949 solely by collecting resources from the families of migrants and later in 1953 it was upgraded to Upper Primary School in 1953. The High School was established in 1979 under the initiative of Mathew Thomas. This institution filled the educational vacuum of Pariyapuram in Angadippuram Panchayath. It was a centre of migration from the farmers of Travancore.[25] At the time of its beginning, the number of students was only 85 and its growth was tremendous in a way that by 1998 its strength increased to 835.[26] This school became a Higher Secondary School in 1998.

The collective initiative of the people of a particular area was instrumental in the beginning of new schools in Malabar. Education societies were formed by the people to apply for new schools and construction of the buildings. The support of the regional political parties played a great role in the establishment of schools in Malabar. The Malappuram district was greatly benefited when Muslim League controlled education department in many years.

Kalladi Education Trust was established to start a school under the leadership of Cheriya Kunjahammad Sahib in Kumaramputhur in Mannarkad in Palakkad district. Under this trust Kalladi High school was started in 1968 with 77 students, five teachers and two non-teaching staff.[27] After thirty years this institution became a higher secondary school with 2750 students, 96 teachers and seven non-teaching staff. This school's achievement was unique in the education history of Palakkad as it received the award for the best school in the district for 20 consecutive years.[28]

Palakkad was one of the early taluks of Malabar district and with the formation of Kerala state in 1956 Palakkad became a district in the Malabar area of Kerala state along with Kozhikode and Kannur. The colonial government had established some premier educational institutions in Palakkad but their effort in the improvement of mass education was not satisfactory. Government Victoria College at Palghat founded in 1866 was one of the earliest colleges in Malabar. Later Madras government laid the foundation for Government College at Chitoor in 1947.

The Christian community of Palakkad was also not behind in their endeavour in setting up educational institutions in Palakkad region. Especially after the formation of the Diocese of Palakkad in 1974 a large number of educational institutions were established in the district.[29] Between 1974 and 2006 various Christian organisations established nine Higher Secondary Schools, 16 High Schools, 30 Upper Primary Schools and 40 Lower Primary Schools in the district.[30] There are 51 Nursery Schools run by different Christian congregations in Palakkad.

Malabar District Board established single teacher schools in Chungakunnu and Talakkani near Kottiyur in 1956. The migrants and Janmies jointly prepared land and small buildings for these schools. Later these schools were upgraded to Upper Primary Schools in 1962. Nair Service Society (NSS) through its Karayogam started an Upper Primary School in 1962 at Kottiyur. Another early institution was a Lower Primary School started by SNDP in 1963 at Kottiyur. A High School was started under Kottiyur church in 1976.

In North Malabar, Peravoor is considered one of the most ancient migration centres of farmers from Travancore. People started their settlement in Thondiyil and Peravoor in 1928. Besides, Peravoor area had several records in the migration history of Malabar. The Primary School at Thondiyil started in 1934 is considered the first full scale school organised by migrants in Malabar. The support of Fr. Ziaro S. J. (the parish priest of Kolayad) to begin this school was very great. Later it became a Higher Elementary school and finally under the able leadership of F. Jose Kuttur it became St. Joseph's High School Peravoor in 1953. The 42nd All Kerala Catholic Conference held in Peravoor in 1960 was a historic event in the migration history of Malabar.

Nirmala Higher Secondary School (H.S.S.) Chemperi, St. Mary's H.S.S. Edoor, Santhome H. S. S. Kolakkad, St. Thomas H.S.S. Thomapuram and St. Joseph's H.S.S., Vayatuparamba are the higher secondary schools in Kannur district which were started as elementary or primary schools by the early migrants of this area. St. Jude's H.S.S. Vellarikundu and St. Sebastian's Velimanam are the higher secondary schools put up by the people after migration.

The steady effort and hard work of the people of Kunnoth finally attained result in 1946 when the government of Madras Presidency granted permission for Lower Elementary School. This was upgraded to an Upper Primary School in 1958. The same building of the church was used for the new school and on Sundays the religious education was given to the children of the locality in the same building. A serious problem of the students was the lack of facilities for secondary education in Kunnoth. The pupil had to travel kilometers crossing rivers and streams to reach the high schools at Edoor or Kilianthara. The students were completely absent in the classes when the monsoon season started.[31] The migrants tried their best to get permission for a high school with the help of political leaders and parish priest.[32] The students who passed seventh standard in 1983 were not allowed to join another school in the assumption that a high school would be sanctioned in the same year. Special arrangements were made for the study of the children in the eighth standard till the sanctioning of the school. It was a great risk because the education of 101 students was illegal. Though the school committee faced several hurdles, at last they acquired sanction for the high school in 1983 itself. The first batch of this high school attained 100 per cent result in 1986. The spacious and big buildings of schools seen in Kunnoth were the result of the foresight of people and parish priests.[33]

The first elementary school in Talipparanmbu area of kannur district was started in Kooveri near Talipparambu in 1906.[34] Later two elementary schools were started in Kanjirakkad and Naduvil. The students of Vayattuparamba faced great difficulty to reach these schools. The first school in Vayattuparamba was St. Joseph's Elementary School, Udumbumcheeta in 1954. It was started in the house of Varghese Pallithara in the beginning and subsequently shifted to new site donated by Lukka Pallithara. He donated two and a half acres of land to the school and the leadership for starting this institution was provided by Mathew Puranganal and I. P. George. This elementary school was upgraded to Upper Primary School in 1958 and it was the first U. P. School in Alakkode and Naduvil zones and students of this area used this school. It was the best in Taliparamba sub-district. The students of this school lost one year as it had no recognition from the government.[35] The final shifting of the school occurred in 1968 in Vayattuparamba. The students of Vayattuparamba had to reach Alakkode, Naduvil and Chapparapadavu to have high school education. A high school was opened in 1982 after several attempts. Fr. Jose Manimalatharappel and a team of migrants took great initiative for this school. A new building was also constructed for the high school by the people. Afterwards a stadium was also put up for the high school. Finally a higher secondary school was started in 2000 with science, commerce and humanities.

The migrants of Udayagiri, situated near to the border of Coorg started an unrecognised school in the building of the church in 1960. The migrants of Udayagiri brought three acres of land for a school and approached the authorities for Primary School.[36] The government sanctioned a school in 1964 and the next year a building was constructed for the school in the place of a small shed. The people constructed another stone building for a U. P. school later. Several early efforts for a school failed to bear fruit and the people were hopeless in their endeavour.[37] They had to wait for 18 long years to get a U.P. school in Udayagiri. Eventually they got upgraded their school to U.P. in 1982 and this school was given the name *Pratheesha* (hope) U.P. school in memory of their long hope for the school.[38]

Kudiyanmala situates in the foothills of Pythalmala, one of the highland areas of Kannur had no facilities for education. The students were forced to go to the school at 15 kilometers distant Chembery, for education. Besides, the journey was very dangerous because students had to cross rivers and streams which had no bridges. So immediately after the construction of the church in 1955 a school was also opened in the same year for education.[39] This private lower primary school functioned under the leadership of Joseph Kurichiyel. The exertion for a recognised school continued by the people till they acquired Fathima Lower Primary school in 1960. It was a great historic event for the people of Kudiyanmala because hundreds of children were eager to join the school. To be precise 340 students joined in the new school within three days of admission in nine standards.[40] The school functioned in the church building till the construction of a new building for the school in 1961. It was upgraded to Upper Primary School in 1964. The continuous effort of the people led to the beginning of Mary Queens High School in Kudiyanmala in 1976.

Around 15 Lower Elementary Schools (L.E.S.) were established under *Taluk* Boards in Wayanad between 1920 and 1940. From the names of schools one could identify the prominent community of a place.[41] The elementary schools in Wayanad had existed at Meppadi, Meenaghadi, Muttil, Pakkam, Kaniyambetta, Panamaram, Mananthavady, Paygattiri and so on. Malabar Local Board was started in 1859 with the objective of promoting primary education in the rural areas. Later Elementary Education Act was passed in 1920 to establish elementary schools.

The L.E.S. in Sulthan Bathery was named Mappila Board School but the schools in Thrissilery, Kallur and Muppainad were called Hindu Board Schools. There were only very meagre facilities for the education in Wayanad. Before independence each taluk had only a few elementary and higher elementary schools run by District and Taluk boards. These schools in Malabar functioned under Madras Education Rules (MER) of Madras government since Malabar was part of Madras Presidency.

By 1960, i.e., within 20 years of active migration the migrants established seven lower primary schools, seven upper primary schools, two high Schools and a teacher Training Institute in Wayanad.[42] Lower Primary Schools of Wayanad in the early years of migration were at Kaniyaram, Kottathara, Nadavayal, Panthallur, Pazhoor, Alattil and Poroor. The Upper Primary schools were established by the poor migrant farmers at Kallody, Kommayad, Mananthavady, Mullankolly, Sulthan Bathery, Thariyode and Thavinjal. The early high schools started by migrants were in Nadavayal and Payyampally. Besides the first Teachers Training Institute in Malabar was started with the contribution of migrants at Mananthavady in Wayanad. According to the estimate in 1966, with setting up of new schools under the eparchy of Thalassery 40,800 students studied in these schools in Malabar.[43]

In 1938 itself the migrants prepared a small shed to give education to their children at Kunthani near Sultan Bathery.[44] Mathai Kuriyakkattil and Kurian Thekkancheriyil took serious steps in the running of this school. Assumption school was the result of the efforts of the early migrants of Sultan Bathery. It was established as a Lower Primary School in 1951 under the initiative of Fr. Zarghese Madathikunnel and was managed by the church. The migrants had carried timber and roof tiles for the school from Beenachi. Voluntary work was also arranged by the people to conduct the earth work for the school. Augusty Puthiyedath, Joseph Vannapram, Mathai Kattarkudi, Mani Pattamana, Thomas Vattakunnel and Xavier Uppuveettil were the leaders who led the people for the construction of the school. The migrants of Kallur and Tottamula made new building for the government Lower Elementary School at Kallur and arranged facilities for the education of students up to the fifth standard.[45] The migrants built a school at Koliyady, but later it was sold to another person.

Table 3.3
District-wise Literacy Rate in Kerala 1971, 1981 and 1991

District	*General Literacy Rate*			
	1961	*1971*	*1981*	*1991*
Cannanore	41.27	55.27	65.74	91.48
Kasargode	–	–	–	82.51
Wayanad	–	47.33	58.33	82.72
Kozhikode	44.88	58.77	70.12	91.1
Malappuram	34.29	47.9	60.5	87.94
Palghat	33.69	46.69	58.00	81.27
Trichur	48.16	61.61	73.59	90.18
Ernakulum	50.33	65.37	76.82	92.35
Idukki	44.33	56.42	67.44	86.94
Kottayam	61.52	72.88	81.66	95.72
Pathanamthitta	–	–	–	94.86
Alleppey	56.90	70.44	78.52	93.87
Quilon	50.49	64.97	74.11	90.47
Trivandrum	45.30	62.54	70.5	89.22

Source: Statistics Since Independence, Department of Economics and Statistics, Thiruvananthapuram, 1998, p. 82.

When large scale migration to Pulpally started in 1950 the students had only very limited facilities for education. So, the migrants of Mullankolly came forward to organise nurseries. A nursery school was started in the house of Mathai Kannamthanath under the supervision of *Masakkuttam*. The aim of the migrants here was to construct a recognised school for their children. Immediately Paily

Vellilamthadathil donated 50 cents of land for the school. During this time the migrants got the help and guidance of the teacher P.C. Thomas to build St. Thomas Aided L.P. School in Mullankolly.[46] Due to the effort of migrants the school got temporary recognition in 1953. Immediately the migrants formed Mullankolly School Committee under the presidentship of Thomas Thekkanattu. The migrants had to face grave situations in the beginning of the school. At first they felt great difficulty in getting a teacher having trained in Malabar educational system. Moreover, a police case was registered in view of the complaint of *Dewaswam* authorities against the President of the School Committee when the migrants cut down some trees for the construction of school building.[47] But nobody could prevent the aspiration of the migrants for a school.

In the *Ulpannapirivu* for the school, migrants gave paddy, lemongrass oil and money to the committee. The wholehearted support to the *Pothupani* for the school helped the timely completion of the construction work of the school. Thus, a fine school building for St. Thomas Aided L.P. School came into existence in 1954. In 1964 it became a U. P. School and later in 1976 it was upgraded to High School. At last in 1991 it became the first aided Higher Secondary School in Wayanad. This pattern of work was almost same in the construction of schools in many parts of migration centres in Wayanad. The growth of this school in the education history of Wayanad was unique.

When Fr. Lukose Poondikulam became the parish priest of Padichira, he started a small school known as *Prabhat Vidhyalayam* with the help of migrants in 1973. Later it was recognised by the government in 1976 and now it became the famous St. Sebastian's U.P. School at Padichira.[48] Due to the educational difficulties of the children at Adikolly, the migrants under the leadership of the church started a new

L.P. School in 1982.[49] P.M. Varkey Pazhayathottathil donated one acre of land for the beginning of G.L.P.S. (Government Lower Primary School) in Marakkadavu in 1955. The educational history of Thariyode was the best example of the vision and hard work of the migrants. The first vicar of Thariyode Fr. Kerubin started St. Mary's L. P. School in 1951[50]. Later in 1952 it was recognised by the government. When Fr. Joseph Hedrian was the vicar of Thariyode church the school was upgraded as U.P. School.

The Malankara Catholic Diocese of Sulthan Bathery paid great attention to the development of education since its inception in 1979. They have started not only educational institutions but also bought schools from others when other managements failed to run the institutions. Mar Baselious U. P. School at Koliyady and St. Thomas A. L. P. School became model institutions after they were taken over by the Diocese. All together five H. S. S., 16 H. S., 19 U.P., 32 L.P. and 30 Nursery Schools now function in this Diocese.[51] St. George U.P. school at Pulpally was an example of an aided school established by the Diocese with the full support of migrants.

K. P. Issac Valayil organised people to start an educational institution in Sultan Bathery.[52] He believed that the social and economic progress of an area could not be achieved without education.[53] He went to Madras to get government sanction for a school. When the school was sanctioned at Sultan Bathery, he proposed the name *Sarvajana* (for all people) for this school and it was the first government high school in South Wayanad. He was a Congress leader among the migrants who worked with Congress leaders of Wayanad, M.K. Jinachandran K. P. Issac had supported M. K. Jinachandran and others to start S. K. M. J. High School at Kalpetta in 1944 and its functioning. He was very proficient in English language and was able to communicate with the British officers very well. His wife Mary Issac joined in this school as a teacher though she had to suffer the adverse climate in Wayanad.[54]

Table 3.4 : Number of Vocational Higher Secondary Schools and Batches in Kerala 2008

	No. of Schools			*No. of Courses*		
Districts	*Govt.*	*Aided*	*Total*	*Govt.*	*Aided*	*Total*
Thiruvanan thapuram	30	11	41	75	36	111
Kollam	20	32	52	51	109	160
Pathanamthitta	10	17	27	35	21	56
Alappuzha	14	7	21	26	51	77
Kottayam	21	10	31	49	26	75
Idukki	22	12	34	54	38	92
Ernakulum	11	5	16	31	15	46
Trissur	26	10	36	64	32	96
Palghat	18	7	25	53	26	79
Malappuram	20	8	28	84	7	91
Kozhikode	24	3	27	64	23	87
Wayanad	8	2	10	44	5	49
Cannanore	18	1	19	52	2	54
Kasargode	19	3	22	44	8	52
Total	**261**	**128**	**389**	**726**	**399**	**1125**

Source: Statistics for Planning 2009, Dept. of Economics and Statistics, TVM, p. 606.

In Kolavayal, the migrants put up St. George Aided Lower Primary school. Its inauguration was done by Paniya chief

Karuman of Koralady Paniya colony.[55] Lower Primary School at Nadavayal was started in 1950. In 1957, this L.P. School has turned into the first High School for the migrants in Wayanad. For the upgradation of this school Fr. Teeshian Pakalomattam, the parish priest of Nadavayal even went to Madras to persuade the government.[56]

In Mananthavady before the establishment of the church the migrants set up a school. Fr. George Kazhukkachalil acquired Aided Lower Primary School in Kaniyaram in 1952 from the management of Church of South India (C.S.I.). In Thavinjal, near Mananthavady a school was started by the migrants in 1942, one of the early schools of migrants in Wayanad.[57] This school was started under the initiative of P. J. Mathai. He was also the first teacher of this school. Later a new building was constructed in the land donated by Kakkuthummel Raman Nair in 1946. The fund for the building and furniture of the school was raised by people and finally it became St. Thomas U. P. School, Thavinjal.

Kasargode area, the northernmost section of Kerala was a part of South Canara district under Madras Presidency in the colonial period. In the wake of the state formation in 1956 Kasargode taluk was bifurcated from South Canara and joined with Kannur district and in1957 it was divided into Kasargode and Hosdurg taluks. Finally on 24 May 1984 these taluks were merged and Kasargode formed as a separate district. Since the new taluk was a part of South Canara district Kannada language had dominance in this district. So, in most of the government and aided schools Kannada medium has been followed along with Malayalam.

One important example of popular initiative in the educational development of Kasargode was the beginning of Durga Higher Secondary School at Kanhangad. There was no amenity for High School education for the students of Kanhangad area till the beginning of this school. The students of Kanhangad had to join six miles distant Raja's High School at Neeleshwaram for their High school education. In tune with the advice of M. C. Nambiar and Molahalli Shiva Rao a public meeting of the people of Kanhangad was convened in 1945 and that meeting decided to start a secondary School in Kanhangad. Some leading figures of Kanhangad formed Hosdurg Education Society in 1946 for the beginning of this school.[58] The chief members of this society C. Kunhiraman Nair, M. C. Nambiar, C. Kunhikannan Nair and K. Narayanan Nambiar contributed Rs 10,000 and more to this society. Krishna Maharaj donated land for the school and Dr B. A. Shenoy permitted the society to start the classes in his own building till the completion of new building the site for the school. Thus, in 1948 the first Upper Primary school in Kanhangad came into existence with three classes (I Form, II Form and III Form).

The unity and urge for education realised the long dream of the people and it was great achievement in the case of the educational development of the people. The entire cost of school building was completely shared by the people of the area. The family of M. C. Nambiar dug a well for the school. The growth of this institution was tremendous in all ways. Within a short period of time the number of students increased from 104 to 1778 by the year 1972.[59] This school also runs classes in Kannada medium in the high school section. The academic standard of this school has been high since the beginning of this institution. This school is ranked as one of the 25 schools in the state on the basis of academic performance in 1959 and 1970. This institution was upgraded to the status of Higher Secondary School in 1998.

Visitation congregation of nuns in Knanaya diocese played a very important role in the education activities of the diocese. Since the beginning of this congregation in 1892 their aim has been educational progress in the society.[60] One fine example of the educational development of a remote area of Malabar due to migration of Knanaya Catholic group was the changes in Panathady near Neeleshwaram in the then South Canara district of Madras Presidency. The Knanaya Catholic diocese of Kottayam had purchased 1800 acres of land for the organised migration and settlement of Knanaya Catholic from Travancore.[61] Professor. V.J. Joseph identified this land for the people and Knanaya bishop Chulaparambil purchased this land in 1942 and the area was renamed as Rajapuram when the migration started in 1943.[62] They started the first school in 1943 itself and the early teachers were P. C. Lukose and Pothan Chempannil.[63] For this school the government sanctioned grant in 1945 with retrospective effect due to the remoteness of the area. It became Holy Family High School, Rajapuram. In 1948, the same management established one U.P. school at Malakkalu and one L. P. school at Ranipuram. In the course of time Knanaya section migrated to many areas of Kanuur started schools there. Sacred Heart High School, Payyavoor, Mary Land High School, Madambam, and three L. P. schools in Payyavoor, Madambam and Kottiyoorvayal are the other schools of Kannur. The Knanaya diocese also started L. P. schools in Kallamala and Mangalagiri in Palakkad. Besides, this management started six unaided schools and 20 nursery schools in different migration centres of Malabar.[64]

Table 3.5 : Number of District-wise Schools in Kerala: 2006-07

	Lower Primary				*Upper Primary*				*High School*				
Districts	*Govt.*	*P. A.*	*P. U.*	*Total*	*Govt.*	*P. A.*	*P. U*	*Total*	*Govt.*	*P. A.*	*P. U.*	*Total*	*G. To.*
Tvm	299	181	27	507	98	101	27	226	119	95	42	256	989
Kollam	268	190	28	486	62	139	16	217	76	131	14	221	924
Pathanamthitta	168	236	22	426	42	84	15	141	48	111	9	168	735
Alappuzha	192	198	21	411	67	77	11	155	58	129	9	196	762
Kottayam	169	268	31	468	67	128	10	205	60	166	22	248	921
Idukki	85	136	10	231	40	63	4	107	56	73	11	140	478
Ernakulam	181	271	33	485	91	103	25	219	87	175	48	310	1014
Trissur	115	381	23	519	55	162	14	231	80	150	31	261	1011
Palghat	194	**349**	**13**	556	63	159	11	233	61	79	33	173	962
Malappuram	350	**477**	**26**	853	113	**223**	**38**	374	82	**84**	**79**	245	1472
Kozhikode	181	**529**	**11**	721	74	**240**	**13**	327	69	**99**	**23**	191	1239
Wayanad	91	**53**	**6**	150	34	**39**	**2**	75	40	**23**	**5**	68	293
Cannanore	114	**608**	**10**	732	76	**280**	**18**	374	83	**80**	**23**	186	1292
Kasargode	141	**115**	**16**	272	72	**72**	**9**	153	77	**33**	**17**	127	552
Total	**2548**	**3992**	**277**	**6817**	**954**	**1870**	**213**	**3037**	**996**	**1428**	**366**	**2790**	**12644**

Source: *Statistics for Planning 2009*, Department of Economics and Statistics, Trivandrum, 2009, p. 592.

(Abbre: Tvm- Thiruvananthapuram, Govt.- Government, P.A.-Private Aided, P.U.-Private Unaided, G. To.-Grand Total)

Government Institutions

But Madras government effected some changes in the education sector of Malabar. The aim of the government was to set up one elementary school in every village having a population 500, a High School in every taluk and college in every district.[65] In this period new District Board High Schools were established in Alathur and Mananthavady. In Koduvally near Thalassery a government Secondary School was also started. The period between 1947 and 1951 government High Schools were set up in Engandiyoor, Cheruvanoor, Chowa, Ayyakkad, Mukkuthala, Edakkulam, Kadachira, Chaliyam, Ponnani, Alanaloor, Chithalancheri, Mullasseri, Keralasseri, Perambra, Vandoor, Mudamkolly, Pattambi, Kallai, Mannarkkad, Thalipparambu, Valapuzha, Nanminda, Naduvannur and Azhikode.

As a part of improving the educational facilities of Malabar special grants were provided to 20 aided elementary schools in Thalassery *Firka* in 1949-50. These special grants were not for the salary of the teacher but to enhance the infrastructure facilities of these schools. Paduppu near Bandadukka was an important area of migration in Kasargode district. Government Lower Primary School, Thavanath was the only school in Paduppu. It was established in 1953 as a single teacher school in the house of Kannan Nair Maliyekkal.[66]

The government established many schools in different parts but their number did not exceed the number of private institutions. Generally the government schools failed to attract the students because of various reasons. The lack of teachers, infrastructure, discipline so on diverted students to nearby aided and unaided schools. According to the estimate of 2006 the total number of government schools in Malabar were 1915 but at the same time the strength of aided schools was 3542. This show the role of private sector in the general education of Malabar. Simultaneously, 353 private unaided schools were providing instruction to the students of Malabar apart from many schools under central scheme and central government.

Schools under Central Scheme

The great fascination of the people regarding English medium in school education resulted the beginning of so many English medium schools in Kerala. These schools were mainly located in the urban or semi-urban areas where there was a domination of middle class people who can pay high fees in these schools. The chief attraction of such schools was their affiliation to Central Board of Secondary Education (CBSE) or Indian Certificate for Secondary Education (ICSE). In CBSE and ICSE schools, they follow the syllabus of central pattern, which is generally considered higher in standard. Besides, strict discipline, dedication and personal attention of the teachers, good infrastructure facilities and so on attract the parents to send their children to these schools. In many areas of Malabar the flow of children from the government and aided schools to CBSE and ICSE was a threat to the job security of teachers in the government and aided schools and even the existence of government schools. The schools directly under central government viz. Kendriya Vidyalaya and Jawahar Navodaya Schools were another group in this category.

Table 3.6 : The Number of CBSE, ICSE, KV and JNV Schools in Malabar : 2003

District	*CBSE*	*ICSE*	*Kendriya Vidyalaya*	*Navodaya Vidyalaya*	*Total*
Palakkad	29	2	3	1	35
Malappuram	40	2	1	1	44

Kozhikode	25	1	2	1	29
Wayanad	8	1	1	0	10
Kannur	30	1	3	1	35
Kasargode	15	2	2	1	20
Total	**147**	**9**	**12**	**5**	**173**

Source: Report on Recognised Unaided Schools in Kerala 2008 Govt. of Kerala, Trivandrum, p. 51.

Organisational Structure of Educational Institutions

After the formation of Kerala state several changes were effected in the education department of Kerala. Kerala Education Act and Kerala Education Rules came into existence in 1st June 1959. The Director of Public Instruction (DPI) is the administrative head of schools in the state.[67] The government started the appointment of IAS officers as DPI since 1960. The conduct of school examination was a great burden for the school section of the department of education under DPI. To formulate a permanent solution to this issue government formulated a separate commissionarate (*Pareeksha Bhavan*) in 1964 at Thiruvananthapuram. Under the Director, in each districts a Deputy Director of Education is appointed to coordinate the Primary and Secondary education in the district. The Deputy Director is the highest authority of general education in the district.

Each revenue district is divided into one or more educational districts and District Education Officers (DEO) are appointed to carry on the day to day affairs of the High Schools and Upper Primary Schools in the district. In Malabar except Wayanad all other districts were divided into two educational districts. The matters regarding creation of new posts in the schools, approval of teachers, passing the salary bill of the teachers, noon feeding of students in the aided Upper Primary and High Schools are the main functions the DEOs of a district. One can appeal to DDE against the decisions of the DEO. In the third layer of the hierarchy educational districts are sub-divided into educational sub-districts under Assistant Educational Officers (AEO). This officer is in charge of large number of Lower Primary Schools in each sub-district. The number of Primary Schools is very high in each district, so the position of AEOs is very important in each district. In Malabar the educational districts were divided into 59 educational sub-districts.[68]

NSS and Education

The performance of the Nairs of Malabar in the field of education was very poor till the second half of twentieth century. The interference of the Nair Service Society (NSS) in the improvement of education in Malabar was not satisfactory.[69] The society is having very few High Schools in Malabar and one of the main centre of NSS institutions is in Palakkad. K. P. T. High School at Ottapalam, NSS High School, Akathethara and NSS High School, Vengassery are the High Schools under NSS in Palakkad district. The only aided High School of NSS in north Malabar is the NSS High School, Alakkode in Kannur. There are only five Upper Primary Schools under NSS in Malabar in both aided and unaided sectors.[70] NSS was able to start only five Lower Primary Schools in Malabar in the above two sectors.[71]

The NSS established one Vocational Higher Secondary School and four Higher Secondary Schools in Malabar.[72] The activities of NSS Karagogams (village units) and Taluk Unions are efficient in Palakkad, Kannur and Kozhikode regions. Alakkode in Kannur was an area of the settlement of migrant Nairs from Travancore. P.R. Ramavarma Raja (Punjar Raja) of Travancore purchased 22000 acres of land in Alakkode in 1937.[73] He sold this land to large number of migrants including Nair migrants. P. R. Ramavarma Raja tried to begin a recognised school in 1954 but the school was started only in 1955 as a single teacher school.[74] By 1958 it became a full fledged government recognised Upper Primary School in Alakkode. It was upgraded to a High School in 1962. Later Higher Secondary School and the management of the school was taken over by NSS.

Table 3.7 : Category and Batches of Higher Secondary Schools in Kerala: 2006 .

Districts	*Govt.*	*Aided*	*Una-ided*	*Total*	*Sci--ence*	*Huma-nities*	*Comm-erce*	*Total*
Thiruvanan-thapuram	74	46	44	164	268	95	108	471
Kollam	55	49	25	129	202	69	79	350
Pathanamthitta	26	36	29	91	127	56	55	238
Alappuzha	41	49	16	106	186	63	70	319
Kottayam	37	59	28	124	221	83	65	369
Idukki	25	26	15	66	86	32	35	153
Ernakulum	63	63	53	179	257	76	129	462
Trissur	62	44	45	151	191	63	92	346
Palghat	55	23	30	108	146	73	76	295
Malappuram	82	44	71	197	224	101	146	471
Kozhikode	62	40	34	136	180	86	86	352
Wayanad	26	11	7	44	57	36	29	122
Cannanore	72	28	27	127	189	73	90	352
Kasargode	55	11	15	81	93	49	49	191
Total	**735**	**529**	**439**	**1703**	**2427**	**955**	**1109**	**4491**

Source : Category and Batches of Higher Secondary Schools in Kerala: 2006.

Ezhava Community

In the educational development of Malabar, Ezhava community played their own role.[75] They began to give more attention to the progress of education after the migration of farmers from Travancore to the high land of Malabar.[76] They were scattered all over Malabar and they set up educational institutions after the formation of the Shakas of Sree Narayana Darma Paripalana (SNDP) Yogam in Wayanad, Kannur and Kozhikode. Some progressive looking and dynamic leaders from Ezhava community initiated individual efforts in the beginning of educational institutions in some remote areas of Malabar.

Some important schools of SNDP in Kozhikode district are situated in Vadakara and Chelannur. An unaided High School was established in Vadakara in 1976. It became a leading school in Vadakara in a short span of time and in 1986 English medium classes were also started in this school. It was upgraded to a Higher Secondary School in 2001 and present strength of the school is 1540. In the field of education Vadakara union of SNDP ranks first with five schools in Malabar. As a part of the delinking of Pre-Degree SNDP Yogam started three Higher Secondary Schools in Malabar. They are S. N. Trust Higher Secondary School (S.N.T.H.S.S.) in Kannur (2000), S.N.T.H.S.S.,Chelannur (2003) and S.N.T.H.S.S., Shornur (2003). In 2000, under the initiative of the Ottapalam union of SNDP a central school known as S.N. Trust Central School was established at Shornur.

Some active members of Ezhava community in Malabar started separate educational institutions. These institutions are not under the control of S. N. Trust or SNDP Yogam administration in Kollam. Such type of two institutions began in Wayanad district of Malabar and they are situated in Puthadi and Pulpally regions. One of the important examples of that sort of institution is the Sree Narayana Higher Secondary School at Puthadi in 1976 and Sree Narayana Lower Primary School at Moodakolly. These institutions are purely under the administration of Puthadi Shaka of SNDP. A managing committee elected from time to time by the members of Poothadi *Shaka* is in charge of the administration of the Sree Narayana Higher Secondary School. It was totally constructed by the Ezhava migrants of Poothadi for their children. P.K. Thankappan Pottananiyil and Anathan Kuzhimullorathu had donated 50 cents of land each for school at Puthadi. These Schools were managed by the respective S.N.D.P. *Shakas* in those areas. Moreover, the people of Ezhava community in Kalluvayal near Pulpally had started another Lower Primary School. Besides, the Ezhava people of Pulpally took strain to start Sree Narayana Lower Primary School at Kappiset. C. K. Raghavan, Changanamattathil, an Ezhava migrant from Vazhithala in Thodupuzha *Taluk* was a prominent leader of S.N.D.P. in Wayanad. He founded the Jayasree High School at Kalanadikolly near Pulpally in 1976.[77]

Muslim Educational Institutions

The reasons of muslims for distrusting western education were same as in the north India. The Muslims were of the opinion that English was "the language of hell" and western education a "passport to hell." As a result of this attitude Muslims were slow to adopt the new system of education and therefore their employment opportunities were also limited. Realising that they were lagging behind, an effort was made with the establishment of Malabar Muslim Educational Association in 1911. Famous social reformer Vakkom Abdul Qadir Moulavi started the "All Travancore Muslim Mahajana Sabha" around the same time. The result of the leadership and awareness led to the opening of many schools by Muslims where there were no government schools in their areas. Madarasthul Muhammadiya in Parappil, Kozhikode is an example of one such school that was established by the Muslim themselves.

Government completed the delinking of Pre-Degree course from the colleges in Kerala in 2000-2001 academic year and in this period large number of Higher Secondary Schools were started in the state under government, aided and unaided sectors of education. The managements of the aided colleges got equal or more number of seats in their High Schools. The government sanctioned High Schools and Higher Secondary Schools simultaneously to some managements who had no High Schools.[78]

Private Unaided Schools

Despite the growing demand for education from people the government failed to meet the demand for quality education in Malabar. This was due to the financial burden of the government for making infrastructure and expenditure for qualified staff in these institutions. This void was filled by the large number of unaided recognised primary, secondary and higher secondary schools in Malabar under various agencies. These institutions are more expensive and cannot be afforded by large section of the society. People who prefer these school pay more for the education of their children and they consider these schools are providing more quality education to their children. Another reason for this preference is that large majority of these schools are affiliated to Central educational bodies like Centre of Board of Secondary Education (CBSE) and Indian School of Secondary Education (ICSE) and follow their curriculum, which is considered as more qualitative than the curriculum followed by the state government.

Vocational Higher Secondary education was introduced in the state during 1983-84. It is designed to prepare skilled work force in the middle level or more group occupations, trade or job after matriculation at plus two level of education. The objective of the course is to enhance individual employability to provide alternative for those pursuing higher education without particular interest or purpose. This course was started by upgrading High School into Vocational Higher Secondary Schools. Higher Secondary course was introduced during the year 1990-91 as a part of delinking pre-degree from colleges to streamline collegiate education. Pre-Degree course was linked to school education and High School were upgraded to Higher Secondary Schools. The administrative control of both Vocational Higher Secondary and Higher Secondary courses was put under separate directorates.

The District Primary Education Programme (DPEP) was introduced in the state during 1994-95 for the educational development with the financial aid of government of India. Later this scheme continued in the name Sarva Siksha Abhiyan (SSA). One important aim of SSA was to universalise elementary education. In recent years the number of such institutions increased all over Kerala because more parents prefer these school instead of government controlled institutions. Many people believe that new pattern in government and aided schools under District Primary Education Programme (DPEP) and subsequent *Sarva Siksha Abhiyan* (SSA) lacks quality in education.

In accordance with the National Policy of Education (1986), District Institute for Education and Training (DIET) were established in 14 districts of the state in 1986. In the field of primary and adult education the DIETs are providing academic and resource support at district level for the development of education.

Recognised and Unaided Schools

Apart from the government and aided schools, there were other two sections of schools in Kerala viz. recognised unaided school and unrecognised schools. In Kerala Education Rules of 1959, Chapter VI, Rules 7 and 8 permits private agencies and individual to start recognised unaided schools upto standard IV.[79] Through this statutory provision any eligible person or a body of persons could establish recognised unaided schools in Kerala in the private sector. Later government started giving recognition of schools beyond standard IV upto standard X as a part of reducing economic burden in aided sector. At the time of the sanctioning of Higher Secondary Schools, recognised unaided Higher Secondary Schools were also sanctioned. The number of such schools in Kerala increased in the period after 1990.

Table 3.8 : The Growth of Recognised Unaided Schools in Kerala 1990-2006

Category	*1990-91*	*2006-07*
HS	111	366
UP	72	213
LPS	134	277
Total	**317**	**856**

Source: Economic Review 2007, Government of Kerala, 2007, p. 58.

This unprecedented growth in the number of unaided recognised institutions was the result of the change of attitude of the middle class. The parents in the middle class were ready to spend money for the education of their children. They also believe that their children would get more individual attention in the unaided recognised schools. Moreover, the English medium of instruction was another attraction of the recognised unaided schools in the society and high income groups.

Unrecognised Schools

Private schools especially in primary section has been a normal stream in the school education of Kerala. These schools are Lower Primary schools functioning without the knowledge of government authorities. In Kerala, especially in the rural areas such schools are attached to Christian churches, SNDP *shakes*, Muslim mosques, religious congregations and organisations as well as private individuals in the state. These schools have no right to conduct public examination in that school as it was not recognised by the government. The management of these schools used to make a tie up with other nearby aided schools and register the name of these students through that school as regular students. So, the students of these unrecognised schools can write the terminal examination of Standard IV and join in government or aided Upper Primary schools in the next year. All the unrecognized schools in the state are working in this *modus operandi*.

Table 3.9 : Number of Unrecognised Schools according to the Year of Starting

Name of Districts	*Before 1991*	*During 91-95*	*During 96-2000*	*After 2000*	*Total*
Thiruvananthapuram	81	71	102	93	347
Kollam	72	57	88	106	323
Pathanamthitta	29	27	42	43	141
Alappuzha	36	24	49	49	158
Kottayam	19	11	25	39	94
Idukki	21	19	29	43	112
Ernakulam	38	25	57	77	197
Trissur	16	15	30	53	114
Palghat	62	38	47	51	198
Malappuram	42	67	92	125	326
Kozhikode	56	47	66	114	283
Wayanad	8	8	13	18	47
Cannanore	33	32	48	58	171
Kasargode	15	28	45	47	135
Total	**528**	**469**	**733**	**916**	**2646**

The number of unaided institutions has been increasing steadily since 1980's. The number of unrecognised schools also increased very fastly in 1990's also and its number increased from 528 in 1991 to 2646 in 2007.[80] The increase in the enrolment of students in unrecognised schools was due to the high income of the people, search for better education, decline of the quality of education in government and aided schools and so on. The parents do not bother about the recognition of the schools because the students could appear for public examination on behalf of other institutions as mentioned earlier. In the district-wise analysis Thiruvananthapuram district has the highest number of schools in the state. In the case of Malabar the number of unrecognised schools are moderately high. Malappuram district has the highest number of such schools in Malabar and this district has second place among the districts in the state. Besides, Malappuram was followed by Kozhikode and Palakkad in the number of unrecognised schools in Malabar.

Table 3.10 : Number of Unrecognised Schools According to Ownership: 2007

Name of Districts	*Proprieto-rship*	*Partne-rship*	*Charitable Society*	*Co-opera-tive Sector*
Thiruvananth-hapuram	122	18	94	8
Kollam	124	9	106	10
Pathanamthitta	47	5	38	6
Alappuzha	38	1	44	7
Kottayam	17		27	6
Idukki	8	4	39	2
Ernakulum	29	3	76	9
Trissur	19	11	39	5
Palghat	54	9	72	5
Malappuram	24	15	130	7

(Contd.)

(Contd.)

Kozhikode	62	15	83	7
Wayanad	3	4	15	
Cannanore	27	9	61	3
Kasargode	26	12	35	4
Total	**600**	**115**	**859**	**79**

From the above table it is clear that charitable societies owned 32.46 per cent of schools in the state. Out of the total 859 unrecognised schools, Malappuram has the highest number of schools run by charitable organisations. In many districts the managements of some schools have provided residential facilities to the students and teachers. In the district-wise analysis 111 schools in the state have residential facilities.[81]

The people of Malabar took education very seriously chiefly after the formation of the state of Kerala. When the existing education with many handicaps including the lack of teacher was not suitable for the general educational progress of Malabar, private institutions took serious interest in the development of education. The migrants established large number of primary, secondary and higher secondary schools in the hilly tracts of Malabar which proved to be a milestone in the educational progress of the extreme rural areas of Malabar. Apart from few individual managements, local committees and few trusts under different communities established schools and they were recognised by the government with grant-in-aid system. Hundreds of unaided CBSE and ICSE schools and many unrecognised private schools played a great role in the educational progress of Malabar. The intervention of the government in the general education through establishing schools was not successful because of various reasons including the usual administrative apathy of the government.

References

1. P.T. Thomas, "Education and Social Mobility: Empirical Issues in Kerala", *Advances in Arts and Ideas*, 4, 1-2 (2008), p. 91.
2. Kathleen Gough, 'Literacy in Kerala' in Jack Goody (ed.) *Literacy in Traditional Societies,* Cambridge, 1975, p. 157.
3. *Rajatha Jubilee Smaranika*, St. Joseph's High School, Kunnoth, 2008, p. 33.
4. T.K. Sebastian, 'Educational and Occupational Mobility among the Migrant Cultivators of Malabar', *Journal of the Institute for Research in Social Sciences and Humanities,* 2,2 (2007), p. 286.
5. 'Kudiyettacharitram: Payyambilly', *Girideepam* 2, 11(1963), Thalassery, p. 24.
6. *Ibid.*, p. 24.
7. *Golden Jubilee souvenir 1949-1999*, St. Sebastian's Church, Koodaranji, 1999, p. 76.
8. *Ibid.*, p.109.
9. The migrants of Pariyapuram near Perinthalmanna in Malappuram brought six sisters from Bethany congregation in Kozhikode to their school when they faced dearth teachers. See *Retirement Souvenir*, St. Mary's High School, Pariyapuram, 1998, p. 43.
10. The post of the then Deputy Inspector of Education was equal to Assistant Education Officer (A.E.O.).
11. In the class visit of the Deputy Inspector of Education the teacher of a particular subject would losse the increment if the student does not answer the question. Due to this reason the salary of the senior teachers was low than the junior teachers. For more information see *Golden Jubilee Souvenir*, St. Joseph's Aided U. P. School, Chempanoda, 2003, pp. 36-37.
12. Govindan and Kunijiraman and Krishna Varrier were the first three teachers who were brought from Kuttuparanmba. *Rajatha Jubilee Smaranika*, St. Joseph High School, Kunnoth, 2008, p. 35.
13. *Suvarna Samvalsaragal*, Fathima Matha Church, Kudiyanmala, 2003, p. 117.
14. Pariyapuram was a centre of migration in Malappuram district. The farmers reached Pariyapuram near Perinthalmanna for agriculture in 1948. They started St. Mary's Lower Primary School in Pariyapuram in 1950 for the education of the children and later it was raised to an upper primary school in 1953. Finally St. Mary's

High School was started in Pariyapuram due to the effort of several people including Mathew Thomas in 1979. The government upgraded this school as higher secondary school in 1998.

15. *Retirement Souvenir*, St. Mary's High School, Pariyapuram, 1998, p. 43.
16. K. Paulose, a teacher.
17. The teachers of Malabar got an additional amount Rs 5 than the teachers from Travancore. At that time the salary of a teacher per month was Rs 45.
18. Many of the famous colleges in Malabar like Victoria College (Palakkad), Malabar Christian College (Kozhikode) and Guruvayurappan College (Kozhikode) were established before independence.
19. The report of the Deputy Director of Education K. J. Lenos and the help of the then Member of Legislative Assembly C. H. Kanaran speeded up the sanctioning of the school. For additional information see *Rajatha Jubilee Souvenir*, St. Mary's High School, Maruthomkara, 1982, p. 107.
20. *Silver Jubilee Souvenir*, St. George High School, Kulathuvayal, 1980, pp. 6-7.
21. *Golden Jubilee Souvenir*, Holy Family U. P. School, Padathukadavu, 1999, p. 22.
22. *Golden Jubilee Souvenir*, St. Joseph's H. S. S., Kodenchery, 2005, p. 58.
23. The speedy growth of this educational institution was due to the hard work of people like C. J. Chacko and E. K. Joseph under the parish priest Mathew Murinjakallel. For a detailed discussion on this topic refer *Golden Jubilee Souvenir 1955-2005*, St. George Church, Vilangad, 2005, p. 36.
24. *Special Edition for the Retirement of P. C. Thomas*, Nirmala Higher Secondary School, Erumamunda, 2010, p. 34.
25. Two farmers Kadenikkad in Chenganassery in South Travancore were the early settlers in Pariyapuram near Perinthalmanna in Malappuram.
26. *Retirement Souvenir*, St. Mary's High School, Pariyapuram, 1998, p. 13.
27. *Sapariya 98*, Souvenir Kalladi High School, Kumaranputhur, Mannarkkad, 1998, p. 22.

28. *Ibid*, p. 22.
29. The eparchy of Palakkad was formed on 27 June 1974 by bifurcating the eparchy of Trissur and eparchy of Thalassery. Palakkad, Mannarkkad, Ottapalam, Melarkode and Alathur are the main areas included in this diocese.
30. *Directory 2006*, Diocese of Palghat, Palakkad, 2006, pp. 83-93.
31. *Rajatha Jubilee Smaranika*, St. Joseph High School, Kunnoth, 2008, p. 35.
32. The demand for a high school developed when Fr. Mathew Villathanam became the parish priest. With the help of the then M. L. A. K. P. Noorudhin the migrants tried for the school.
33. The fund raising activity for the Golden Jubilee building in 1996 started in 1992 onwards. *Suvarna Jubilee Smaranika*, St. Thomas Church, Kunnoth, 1992, p. 11.
34. *Platinum Jubilee Smaranika*, St. Joseph's Forane Church, Vayattuparambu, 2007 p. 73.
35. *Ibid.*, p. 75.
36. Under Fr. Augustine Kizhakkarakkad the attempt of the people to obtain permission for the U. P. School miscarried three times.
37. *Pythrukam, Suvarna Jubilee Smaranika*, St. Mary's church, Udayagiri, 2007, p. 81.
38. The migration of farmer to Kudianmala started in 1951 with the coming of Cherian Kattakayam. For additional information see *Suvarna Samvalsaragal*, Fathima Matha Church, Kudiyanmala, 2003, pp. 39-40.
39. *Suvarna Samvalsaragal*, Fathima Matha Church, Kudiyanmala, 2003, p. 121.
41. The L. E. S. in Sulthan Bathery was named Mappila Board School but the schools in Thrissileri, Kallur and Muppainad were called Hindu Board Schools.
42. The schools that existed in Gudallur *Taluk* (Tamil Nadu) are included in this list because it was migration centre along with Wayanad.
43. *Girideepam, Special issue, Thalassery,* 1968, p. 57.
44. The early teachers of this school were the senior migrants themselves and its work was not satisfactory till the permanent appointment of a teacher in 1949. An ex-serviceman, Krishnan from Palakkat came forward to give education to the students and he was

given a small amount as salary by the migrants per month. When it was started, the school had only seven students and by 1950 it increased to 22. Later the migrants could not manage this school so it was handed over to the government and now it became the Government Lower Primary School, Kunthani. Information received from John Xavier, Uppuveettil House, Kunthani, Sulthan Bathery.

46. He was migrant from Pavaratti near Thrissur. He joined in the United Aided Elementary School, Pulpally as a teacher. He was a very efficient organiser who played a leading role in the development of Pulpally.

47. According to the M.P.P.F. Act of 1946 cutting of trees more than three feet diameter was a crime. He had to go underground for several days and he was finally freed by the court without punishment. For more details see, *Souvenir of Pulpally Immigration...*, Mullankolly, *op.cit.*, pp. 20-22.

48. *Rajatha Jubilee Smaranika*, St. Sebastian's Church, Padichira, 1998, p. 41.

49. The school was known as Deva Matha L. P. School and later it became an aided school.

50. In the beginning this school functioned inside the church. The first teacher was Mathai Karuthedath, a migrant farmer from Kuravilangad.

51. *Directory, The Syro-Malanakara Catholic Major Archiepiscopal Church*, Sulthan Bathery, 2006, pp. 195-200.

52. K. P. Issac migrated from Kizhakkambalam near Ernakulam in 1939 and settled near Sultan Bathery. He was one of the few graduates among the migrants and popularly known as 'Issac *mash*' ('Teacher Issac'). His daughter Valsala Scaria was the first lady veterinary doctor in Wayanad.

53. He had approached several prominent people of Sultan Bathery to start an educational institution. He did not get encouragement from them. Information given by M. K. Joseph, Madathikudiyil, Koliyady, Sulthan Bathery.

55. This inauguration was on 5 June 1979.

56. Mariadas Kuzhippil, *C.M.I. Sabhayude Malabar Kudiyettam*, Cochin, 2001, p. 80.

57. This school was started in the house of one of the *Janmies* of that area named Elampool Sankaran Nambiar and that school functioned only three months in that house.

58. *Silver Jubilee Souvenir*, Durga High School, Kanhangad, 1973, p. 13.
59. *Op. cit.*, p. 16.
60. *Visitation Congregation Centenary Souvenir1892-1992*, Kottayam, 1992, p. 35.
61. The Knanaya Catholics are Syrian Christians but they claim separate ancestry from 72 families brought to Kerala from Syria by Thoma of Knana in A.D. 345.
62. V. J. Joseph was the professor of St. Aloshiyas College, Mangalore and President of Knanaya Catholic Congress. They purchased 1800 acres of *Janmam* land from Kakkattumadathil Kovilakam in Hosdurg taluk. *Malabar Knanaya Kudiyetta Suvarna Jubilee Smaranika 1943-1993*, Kannur, 1993, p.11.
63. The other teachers of this school were M. J. Lukka, K.C. Thomas, K. M. Mariyamma and Mathai Kanayamparambil.
64. *Malabar Knanaya Kudiyetta Suvarna Jubilee Smaranika 1943-1993*, Kannur, 1993, p.119.
65. *Anjukollathe Nettangal-Malabar District*, Information and Publicity Department, Government of Madras, Madras, 1951, pp. 36-37.
66. *Consecration Souvenir*, St. George Church, Paduppu, 2003, p. 117.
67. The head of the education department is Education Minister. Under the minister General Education Secretary coordinate the administration of education department. The Director of Public Instruction (DPI) is also under the supervision of General Education Secretary.
68. The number of educational sub-districts in Malabar are the following. They are Palakkad-12, Malppuram-17, Kozhikode-15, Wayanad-3, Kannur-15 and Kasargode-7.
69. *Nair Service Society* : Nair Service Society is a registered charitable society founded in the year 1914 by late Mannath Padmanabhan. He was the legendary social reformer, educationist and visionary among the Nair of Kerala. NSS had played a very great role in the social and educational development of Travancore.
70. The NSS U.P. Schools are situated in Alakkode, Ottapalam, Uppada, Manjeri and Kalpetta.
71. The L. P. Schools of NSS are situated in Uppada, Alakkode, Majeri, Kozhikode and Kalpetta.
72. NSS VHS School at Ottapalam and NSS Higher Secondary Schools are functioning in Alakkode, Kozhikode, Manjeri and Kalpetta.

73. It is a Brahmasam land under Melppalli Brahmin family near Thalipparambu in Kannur. For more information see Kuravilangad Joseph, *Konippadikal*, Kozhikode, 1991, pp. 533-534.
74. *Suvarna Jubilee Smaranika 1995-2005*, St. Marys Forane Church, Alakkode, 2005, pp.162.
75. Tiyyar Malabar Association established in Kozhikode by C. Krishnan in 1925 was the first association of Tiyya community in Malabar. Its local variations were Ezhava Mahajana Sabha, Palakkad and Sree Narayana Guru Smaraka Samajam, Ponnani. M. C. Sankara Narayanan was the founder of this Samajam in 1925. It had 40 Shakas and 12000 members and later it came to be known as Malabar SNDP Yogam.
76. For more details on the migration of Ezhava community from Travancore to Malabar and their role in the development of education See Joshy Mathew, 'Agrarian Migration in Wayanad: A Socio-Historical Study' (Unpublished Ph.D thesis submitted in Kannur University, pp. 283-284.
77. He was the first secretary of the Wayanad Union of S.N.D.P. in 1966. For more details see *Niranghal Chalicha Sheshippukal*, C.K. Raghavan Memorial College of Teacher Education, Kalanadikolly, Pulpally, 2007, pp. 5-6.
78. St. Mary's Higher Secondary School in Sulthan Bathery under Syrian Orthodox Eparchy of Sulthan Bathery and Marthoma Higher Secondary School, Chungathara near Nilambur under Marthoma Christian religious section.
79. A Report on Recognised Unaided Schools in Kerala 2008, Government of Kerala (Report prepared by A. A. Baby), Thiruvananthapuram, 4.
80. *Report of Survey on Unrecognised Schools in Kerala*, Department of Economics and Statistics, Thiruvananthapuram, 2007, p.13.
81. *Report of Survey on Unrecognised Schools in Kerala*, Department of Economics and Statistics, Thiruvananthapuram, 2007, p. 4.

4
Higher Education in Malabar

The facilities for higher education were very meagre in Malabar till the first half of the twentieth century. The people of Malabar had no interest in higher education because of various reasons. The Marumakkathayam form of family among the higher castes, landlord-peasant social and economic system, lack of job opportunities in government and private sector and so on ruined the interest of the people in higher education. A very small segment of people who wished to have education depended chiefly on the colleges in Bombay, Madras, Mangalore and Mysore cities. The British government in Malabar for a very long period neglected the promotion of higher education as they were preoccupied with revenue collection and suppression of the resistance of national movement.

The University of Madras, established in 1857 was the only university in south India and all the colleges in the Madras Presidency were affiliated to this university.[1] All colleges in Malabar continued their affiliation in this university till the formation of Kerala state in 1956. After that these colleges were affiliated to Kerala University. Many Malayali youths proceeded to Madras and elsewhere to complete their higher education in the nineteenth century.[2]

Table 4.1 : Number of Students under University Education in Malabar 1867-1883

Years	*University Pupil*
1867-68	10
1872-73	32
1877-78	55
1882-83	149

Source: William Logan, *Malabar Manual,* Vol. 1, New Delhi, p. 106.

For several decades Kerala had only one university namely, Travancore University. It was established in 1937 and later known as Kerala University.[3] Till the formation of the University of Calicut in 1968 all the colleges in Kerala were affiliated to Travancore University.[4]

The great effort of the people of Malabar resulted in the beginning of largest number of colleges under University of Calicut. Consequently a new university was started in Malabar at Kannur by bifurcating University of Calicut in 1996 known as Kannur University. Even after the formation of this new university the University of Calicut holds first place in the number of affiliated colleges.

Education Before Independence

In Malabar, the students after completing the High School education joined in the colleges for Intermediate course. After passing Intermediate, candidates sought admission for the degree course. After the completion of intermediate the students joined for F.A. (Fellow of Arts) and later it was called B.A. (Bachelor of Arts). The higher education scenario in Malabar also began to show a change with the arrival of missionaries. The Christian missionaries started many higher educational institutions in Malabar and later some other prominent sections established educational institutions in Malabar. The beginning of Malabar Christian College had opened up a new chapter in the field of education. It provided a chance to the people of Malabar for the first time for higher education. The college can boast of a line of distinguished educationalists as principals from Germany, England and Malabar. It is the oldest and foremost arts and science college in Malabar. Its humble origin was in the form of a Primary School opened by Basel Evangelical Mission at Kallayi in 1848. Later it was shifted to Calicut city and in 1878 it became a High School. This institution secured the recognition of the University of Madras as a Second Grade College in 1907. This was a landmark in the higher education scenario of Malabar. During the academic year of 1960-61 the number of students in the college was 689 under various courses. A hostel for outstation students also functioned under this college was an attraction to the students of all districts of Malabar.

The first native institution which later become a second grade college was a school commenced by the royal family of the Zamorins of Calicut in 1877. The name of this institution was *Kerala Vidhyasala*. It was recognised and elevated to the status of a Second Grade College in 1879 by University of Madras. This institution was rechristened as Zamorins College in 1900 and in 1952 it became a first grade college and assumed a new name Guruvayurappan College.

The beginning of this giant educational institution in Palakkad in Malabar was in the form of a Rate School in 1866.[5] This Rate School became Government High School in 1877 and in the year 1888 it was raised to the rank of a Second Grade College and the government handed over its management to the Municipal Council of Palakkad. The name of British queen Victoria was given to this college to commemorate the golden jubilee of queen's accession to the throne in 1887.[6] The students of this college joined in Fellow of Arts (F.A.) course and the college was affiliated to Madras University. In the first batch 27 students appeared in F.A. Exam. A school started by another missionary namely, Edward Brennen in Thalassery became the very renowned Govt. Brennen College in Thalassery.

Development of Higher Education after Independence

The higher education received great impetus in India chiefly after independence. The recommendation of Kothari Commission 1964-66 provided a vision to the university education. He said to seek and cultivate new knowledge; to provide the right kind of leadership in all walks of life; to provide society with competent men and women; to provide for equality and social justice are the chief objectives of higher education in India.[7] In the case of Kerala government promoted private sector with much importance in the establishment of higher educational institutions.

Rural Colleges

Rural colleges were started in Malabar by the Madras government in 1950. The aim of these colleges was to give higher education to the students in the rural areas who were not able to study in High Schools. The pupil who passed ESLC (Elementary School Leaving Certificate) and completed 19 years could join in Rural Colleges. The first Rural College was established at Vadakara in 1950. The lecturers of these colleges were guest faculties from High Schools and Colleges, doctors, advocates and so on. The faculty taught the students different subjects in Rural colleges.

Aided Colleges

The regional committees formed by people in various parts of Malabar for putting up higher educational institutions also played an important role in the educational development of Malabar. The establishment of Farook College was a turning point in the progress of modern education among the Mappila community in Malabar. This institution has been run by the Farook College Managing Committee elected annually by Rouzathul Uloom Association started by several progressive thinking Muslim individuals of Calicut.[8] This institution has been functioning as the chief education centre of Mappila Muslims of Malabar. There is hardly any village today in the Malabar area which does not have a few alumni of the Farook College institutions.[9] In the beginning this college was also started under the University of Madras and at present it is the biggest residential Post Graduate institution under the University of Calicut.

Another prominent college established by a committee in Malabar was Sir Syed College, Thaliparamba in Kannur. Kannur District Muslim Educational Association (KDMEA), an association founded by a group of prominent Muslims in 1967 as a Junior College and in the course of time the same became a post graduate institution in north Malabar under Kannur University. The proclaimed aim of the college is the educational and moral betterment of the Muslim minority.[10] Another committee of the same nature was Tirurangadi Muslim Orphanage Committee which founded Pocker Sahib Memorial Orphanage (PSMO) College in 1968 as junior college at Tirurangadi in Malappuram. The college of this registered committee was upgraded as a first grade college in 1972 affiliated to Calicut University. In 1980, the former junior college became a post graduate college having nine degree courses and six post graduate courses. A special weightage has been given to the education of orphans in the Muslim community.

One notable institution in Malabar is St. Joseph's college, Devagiri in Calicut. The genesis and efflorescence of this college owe to the Carmelites of Mary Immaculate (CMI), a Christian religious congregation.[11] Fr. Shabor Vallavanthara and Fr. Hormice Perumalil understood the need of a first grade arts college for the people of Malabar chiefly for the Catholic emigrants in the region. Moreover a large number of priests including the chiefs of the Kottayam Province of the CMI took great interest in the beginning of this college. In 1955, they brought 77 acres of land in Calicut for the college and constructed required buildings for the college to get affiliation from the University of Madras. This college was finally opened in June1956 with the first batch of 200 Pre-University students and 20 BA students.[12]

The higher education of women in Malabar was a neglected area till the beginning of a few women's colleges. The sisters of the Apostolic Carmel established Providence Women's College in Calicut in 1952. This was a dream come true for the young women in the Malabar region who had to otherwise go as far as Mangalore or Madras in search of a women's college. The humble beginning of this college was in the small building of Providence High School in Calicut with 67 students. Now the college has grown into a full-fledged higher education centre for women with more than 1300 students. Providence Women's College was the result of the efforts of a group of dedicated sisters headed by Mother Gabrielle. Thus, this college opened a new chapter in the annals of Malabar, as its first women's college.[13] The college was first affiliated to the Madras University. Later the affiliation was shifted to the Kerala University and University of Calicut successively. Today this college offers two PG courses, 12 UG courses several certificate courses.

The first aided college in Wayanad was St. Mary's College, Sulthan Bathery. This was the result of the vision of Fr. Mathai Nooranal. He formed a local committee for the college and as the secretary of the committee he applied for a college in 1965 to the University of Kerala through the Bishop of Malankara Orthodox Church.[14] The committee received revenue land for the college under lease. The migrants donated money for the beginning of the college and it started functioning in 1965 itself.[15] The college started hostels for the students considering the geography of Wayanad, consequently the students from all over Wayanad stayed in the hostel for the study. Not only the children of migrants but also students of natives and tribal people received higher education from this institution. It was upgraded to a degree college in 1970 and in 1984 it became the first Post Graduate College in Wayanad[16].

Another college in a migration centre in Wayanad was Pazhassi Raja College in Pulpally. It was the result of the concerted effort of a group of migrant farmers in Pulpally under the leadership of T.U. Jacob[17]. They formed a society known as 'Pazhassi Raja Education Society' to begin a college in 1982. He started the college in the same year in a small shed in Pulpally.

The Diocese of Mananthavady very seriously addressed the issue of educational backwardness of north Wayanad especially in the case of higher education. The effort under the leadership of the first bishop of this diocese, Rev. Jacob Thoomkuzy led to the establishment of Mary Matha College in 1995. This aided college filled the gap of higher education of north Wayanad. This college was very beneficial for the tribal population of north Wayanad. Now this college offers five Under Graduate courses and one Post Graduate course. Moreover, this college is a research centre of Mathematics and Zoology under Kannur University.

The colleges started due to the hard work of migrants offered great opportunity to the tribal population of Wayanad. Before the beginning of these colleges the tribal students had no idea of higher education in Wayanad. When we compare the aided colleges with the government colleges in the case of tribal students intake, the position of aided college is much better. The following estimate proves this fact:

Table 4.2 : Student Details of Colleges in Wayanad 2000

Sl. No.	*Name of College*	*Status*		*Student Strength*			
			Total	*Male*	*Female*	*S. C.*	*S.T.*
1	Govt. College, Kalpetta	Govt.	418	272	146	28	29
2	Govt. College, Mananthavady	Govt.	386	205	181	28	42
3	St. Mary's College Sulthan Bathery	Private	1692	698	994	89	208
4	Pazhassi Raja College, Pulpally	Private	804	372	432	61	32
5	Mary Matha College Mananthavady	Private	258	108	150	33	52
6	W.M.O., College, Muttil	Private	217	107	110	7	2

Source: Janakiyasuthrana Prasthanam,- Wayanad Jilla, District Planning Department, Kalpetta, 2000, p.167.

The beginning of Nirmalagiri College at Kuttuparamba in Kannur in 1964 was a landmark in the effort to eliminate the educational backwardness of North Malabar in higher education. Pre-degree course was started at first and later a few degree courses were begun in 1967. In the beginning this college was under Kerala University and eleven teachers, five non-teaching staff worked and 397 students studied in this college during that period. The present huge building of this college was constructed under the leadership of Fr. John George Vadakkumula with the financial support of common people in 1970. This college showed a tremendous growth and at present this college has ten degree courses, two postgraduate courses.

The first regular college started by migrants in Kasargode district in Malabar was St. Pious X College, Rajapuram. Though the people of Rajapuram had many opportunities for school education, there was lack of facility for higher education in this colony of migration. The authorities realised the need of a regular college in Rajapuram and they purchased 25 acres of land for the college. Without the recognition of the university the Knanaya diocese constructed a huge building for the college in 1990 and started pre-degree course in the college as a parallel institution in 1990-91. In the succeeding years degree courses were started in the college. In 1995 the government and university recognised this college. Now-a-days it became one of the prominent colleges in North Malabar with a student strength of 523.[18]

Government and universities in Malabar neglected research in social science disciplines. This wide gap in higher education was filled by Institute for Research in Social Science and Humanities at Kuttuparamba in Kannur in 2002. Kannur University recognised this institute as its research centre in 2004. This institute offer Ph.D. course in History, Malayalam, Economics and so on. Indira Gandhi National Open University (IGNOU) also recognised this institute as a research centre in Kerala.

Universities in Malabar

The educational backwardness of higher education in Malabar was a great concern to the people and political leaders of Malabar. The demand for a university in Malabar was not considered by the early governments of Kerala and the then largest single party in Malabar, Muslim League was in the forefront of this demand. At the time of the EMS Namboodiripad's tenure of third ministry in Kerala, a prominent Muslim League leader C. H. Muhammad Koya was the minister of education and he had great interest in the establishment of a university in Malappuram because of its retarded status in education.[19] Due to his special interest Calicut University was established in Malappuram district in 1968. This university had jurisdiction over the six districts of Malabar and Trissur district in the central part of Kerala.

The second university in Malabar is Kannur University founded in 1996.[20] The aim of the university was to provide a fillip to the development of higher education in Kasargode and

Kannur districts and the Mananthavady taluk of Wayanad district. The Act of this university envisages establishment of teaching and research campuses at Kannur, Kasargode, Mananthavady, Payyannur, Thalassery and Kanhangad to promote advanced knowledge in Science and Technology, Arts, Humanities and other relevant disciplines.

Table 4.3 : Arts and Science Colleges under Various Universities in Kerala 2007

	University	*Govt.*	*Aided*	*Unaided*	*Total*
1.	Kerala University	9	37	15	61
2.	University of Calicut	17	45	58	120
3.	M. G. University	7	56	54	117
4.	Kannur University	6	12	26	44
	Total	**39**	**150**	**153**	**342**

Source: Mathrubhoomi Uparipadanam Directory, Kozhikode, 2006, pp. 196-212

Muslim Education Society (MES) and Higher Education in Malabar

The largest number of colleges among the districts of Malabar is Malappuram and most of these colleges are under the management of Muslim community. The Mappila Muslims of Malabar were very backward in the field of modern education in the colonial period and they failed to seek admission in the government colleges and colleges run by other communities in the post-independence period. This was due to the lack of support from the society and age old backwardness of Mappilas in education. But in the religion-wise growth rate of population of Muslims in Malappuram was high in 1961-71. The Muslim growth rate of population in Malappuram was 48 per cent while the growth rate among Hindus was 13 per cent in the same period.[21]

The attitude of orthodox Muslims in the higher education of children was not favourable and they vehemently opposed the education of women after school studies. Regarding this situation P. K. Abdul Gafoor denounced this attitude and said 'many people expressed the view that Muslim women do not need secular education at all. Some others express willingness to permit women up to eighth standard and a few others are liberal to give them education till tenth standard. Did *Allah* make any demarcation in the case of women's education?'.[22] Due to the hostile attitude of Muslim general public to Higher education, students of this community generally avoided college education. They did not strengthen their facilities for education and were even averse to utilise existing government colleges for education. But very few progressive Muslim students went to Aligarh Muslim University for their education.

Predecessors of Muslim Education Society

The first organisation in Malabar aimed at the progress of education and modernisation of Muslims in Malabar was Calicut Muslim Association. C. P. Kunjahammad Sahib, K. Muhammad Kutty, M. A. Abdullah and A. V. Muhammad were the foremost leaders of Calicut Muslim Association.[23] The students who studied in Aligarh Muslim University had received much cosmopolitan exposure and realised real educational backwardness of Muslims in Kerala especially Malabar. Many of them returned to Malabar with the idea of the advancement of Muslim community. Some of the broad members were old students of Aligarh Muslim University like P. K. Abdul Ghafoor, P. K. Abdullah, K. M. Muhammad Ali, K. M. Bahaudin and so on. Many of them completed their Bachelors and Master's degrees in law, history, economics and other subjects. They formed Aligarh Old Boys Association in 1960 and its main leaders were P. K. Abdul Ghafoor and K. M. Bahaudin. Their chief aim was to help Muslim students in their education as a part of their work they financially supported the poor students in Farook College. Many of these leaders financially supported the Muslim students of medical and engineering colleges in Malabar but in the course of time the unity and common aim of community development led to formation of a great organisation in Malabar.

The hostile attitude shown in secular education was absent in oriental education among the Muslims. They established many Arabic Colleges in different parts of Kerala especially in Malabar.

Rouzathul Uloom Arabic College, Farook; Madeenathul Uloom Arabic College, Kondotti, Sulla Musalam Arabic College, Areekkode and Mounathul Islam Arabic College, Ponnani are the important institutions in Malabar. But the Mappila community had to wait till 1948 for their first modern arts and science college in Malabar i.e. Farook College near Kozhikode.

Muslim Education Society

The formation of Muslim Educational Society (MES) was a landmark in the educational progress of Muslims in Kerala. It was formed in Kozhikode on 10 September 1964 by a group of progressive Muslims in Malabar. P. K. Abdul Ghafoor, M. A. Abdullah, Muhammad Kutty, C. P. Kunjahammad, K. M. Bahaudin, A. P. Ibrahim Kunju and A. V. Muhammad with the aim of providing financial assistance to Muslim students for their education. P. K. Abdul Ghafoor became the first president of MES and under his leadership MES became a great Muslim institution in India.[24] Since 1972 district and block committees of MES were started and its activities began to penetrate into the grassroot level of Muslim community in Kerala. Within a very short time MES gained the respect and credibility in the society. MES announced Rs 25,000 scholarship in the very next year of its formation and initially patron members contributed Rs. 1000 each to raise this amount. Moreover, MES announced that within four years the scholarship amount would be raised to one lakh rupees in every year by making an annual increase of Rs 25,000[25]. Within a few months official membership in MES increased from 100 to 822 and out of them 186 patron members contributed Rs 1000 each,146 life members donated Rs 600 and the rest of the members contributed to the organisation according to their ability[26].

Their main source of money was the donation from the people. One of their important ventures was providing books and dress to the Muslim children in the schools. Between 1965 and 1967 MES apart from the regular donation of Rs 75,000 provided school dress for 3000 students and text books for 1000 students in Malabar.[27] The supply of scholarship was a great motivation and help to the Muslim students in Malabar but the leaders felt the handicap of lack of higher educational institutions for Muslims in Malabar. Though MES was ready to give more educational scholarship to students they had no seats for the admission of students especially in higher education sector. During that time MES had no resources like land and money for the beginning of a college. But unexpectedly MES president P. K. Abdul Ghafoor got an offer of enough land and one lakh rupees from Cheriya Kunjahammad Sahib at Kalladi near Mannarkkad for setting up of a college there in 1966. Abdul Ghafoor suddenly accepted the offer and after overcoming all the hurdles put up MES Kalladi College in 1967. For this college Kunju Muhammad Haji Valayadi donated 12 acres and Kunjapputti Sahib Thavalappara donated two acres of land to the college. These generous contributions of Muslims for the beginning and maintenance of educational institutions were an example of attitude of Muslims towards education. This is the only college in Palakkad district under Muslim management. In 1971, this junior college was upgraded to a degree college and degree courses in History, Economics, Mathematics, Commerce, Islamic history, Chemistry and Physics were started in the college. It became a Post Graduate college since 1978 and offered PG courses in Commerce and History. Now it has become a leading arts and science college in Malabar.

The educational activities of MES were very fast under its first president in Malabar. For the commencement of another MES college at Ponnani P. K. Abdul Ghafoor applied the same method as in the case of first college. Ponnani in Malappuram was very backward in higher education and while inaugurating Ponnani Muslim Educational Society MES president came out with the proposal of a college in Ponnani and encouraged the people to emulate the example of the beginning of MES Kalladi college in Palakkad. MES promised that if they collected rupees one lakh and enough land MES would be able to start a college within one year. The people of Ponnani took this challenge and raised more than one lakh of rupees and it was given to MES for the construction of a college at Ponnani in 1967. Besides, the enthusiastic people acquired 35 acres of land in Ponnani under lease from the government with the help of then minister E. K.

Imbichibava. MES kept its word by starting MES Ponnani College in 1968. This under graduate college with degree courses in Geology, Economic, Commerce, Zoology and Physics was upgraded to a post graduate college in 1979 and PG courses were started in Economics, Commerce and Physics.

Mampad Junior College was an example of the interest of some of the Muslims in Eranad taluk had in the development of higher education in Muslim dominated area in Malabar. Due to his personal interest famous Muslim scholar C. N. Ahammad Moulavi secured government permission for the beginning of a college. Athal Moideen (Adhikari) in Mampad donated 25 acres of land in Mampad Panchayath and Muslims of Mampad formed Eranad Muslim Educational Association for the beginning of this school. Thus, the second college under Muslim management started functioning in 1965. The lack of experience in running a college and financial crisis had created several hindrance in the functioning of the college and finally association stopped the functioning of this college in 1969. To save this college, that had been existing in an educationally backward Muslim area the managing committee expressed its willingness to handover the college to MES, which proved its mettle in successfully running colleges in Malabar.

The executive committee of MES discussed this proposal of the takeover of the college but a large majority of the members objected this suggestion chiefly on the basis of financial burden. Some members warned that the new college would be burden to MES and this would create financial exigency to the society and pressured in the committee to abandon the proposal. But P. K. Abdul Ghafoor took a different view in this issue. His view was that if MES hesitates to take over this institution it would be a great loss to the Muslims in Malabar. While the matter was put to vote in executive committee. Abdul Ghafoor used his casting vote in favour of the take over of Mampad College. Thus, in 1969 MES took over Mampad College from Eranad Muslim Educational Association and from 1970 the progress of the college was very rapid. This college changed the educational history of Eranad Taluk in Malappuram district. In 1970, this college was upgraded to a U.G. college and degree courses in Mathematics, Zoology,

Chemistry, Commerce, Arabic and Economics and post-graduate courses in Zoology, Chemistry, Mathematics, Arabic and Economics were started 1978. MES College in Mampad became a college of the largest number of Muslim students in Kerala in 1976 and it was 63 per cent of total number of students in the college[28].

The administration of MES colleges was handled by local committees. Each college has been working under a local committee consisting of a president, vice-president, secretary, joint secretary, treasurer, correspondent and legal advisor. Such committees were very helpful for the resource mobilisation and local functioning of the college.

Table 4.4 : Enrolment of Students in the MES Colleges in Malabar 1967-1994

Name of College	*No. of Students in the Beginning*	*No. of Students in 1993 -94*	*No. of Muslim Students in the beginning*	*No. of Muslim Students in 1993 -94*	*No. of Muslim Girls in the beginning*	*No. of Muslim Girls in 1993-94*
MES College, Kalladi	286	2279	90	1332	9	426
MES College, Ponnani	215	2199	70	965	10	317
MES College, Mampad	269	1832	110	1143	4	432
MES Women's College, Kozhikode	-	935	-	-	-	328

Source: Compiled from *MES Charithram 1964-94*, Calicut, 1994, pp. 77-92.

Another contribution of MES in the education field of Malabar was the resource mobilisation from inside and outside the country. For the construction of college buildings and hostels MES obtained grants from UGC and central government in large scale. At the time of the takeover of Mampad College MES acquired rupees one lakh from Nizam's Trust of Hyderabad. MES College Ponnani arranged rupees 15 lakhs for the construction of college hostel. MES encouraged rich community members to donate money for the construction of different building in the college. Besides, UGC's fund was for the special coaching of students appearing for medical and engineering courses in MES college Kalladi.

Table 4.5 : Category-wise Arts and Science Colleges in Kerala 1968, 1997 and 2007

Districts	*1968*			*1997*			*2007*		
	Govt.	*Private*	*Total*	*Govt.*	*Private*	*Total*	*Govt.*	*Private*	*Total*
Thiruvananthapuram	3	11	14	7	12	19	8	12	20
Kollam	-	13	13	1	12	13	1	12	13
Pathanamthitta	-	-		-	9	9	-	9	9
Alappuzha	-	13	13	-	12	12	-	12	12
Kottayam	-	19	19	1	20	21	1	21	22
Idukki	-	-		2	6	8	2	6	8
Ernakulam	1	14	15	4	21	25	4	21	25
Trissur	-	13	13	3	17	20	3	17	20
Palghat	3	5	8	3	7	10	4	9	13
Malappuram	-	-	-	3	9	12	3	8	11
Kozhikode	2	10	12	6	8	14	6	8	14
Wayanad	-	-	-	2	4	6	2	4	6
Cannanore	2	6	8	2	9	11	2	9	11
Kasargode	-	-	-	3	2	5	3	2	5
Total	**11**	**104**	**115**	**37**	**148**	**185**	**39**	**150**	**189**

Source: Data compiled from *Statistics Since Independence*, Department of Economics and Statistics, Thiruvananthapuram, 1998, p. 91 and *Statistics for Planning 2009*, D.E.S, TVM, p. 07.

Colleges under S.N. Trust

When R. Sankar was the general secretary of SNDP Yogam he took great interest in the educational development of the community.[29] He had special interest in the beginning of colleges in Malabar. He collected money from all *Shakas* of Kerala for beginning educational institutions.[30] For the effective administration of all educational institutions R. Sankar proposed the establishment of an autonomous trust in 1945.[31] This shows the great vision in the educational improvement of Ezhava community. Finally Sree Narayana Trust (S.N. Trust) was established in 1952 and he became the founder secretary of the trust.

The first college of Ezhava community in Malabar was S. N. College in Kannur established in 1960. R. Sankar was the founder manager of this college and he encouraged the people to donate resources for this college. In most of the colleges SNDP Yogam formed Regional Development Council (RDC) under a president to look after the immediate requirements of the college. This system of institution could acquire local financial and material help for the development of the colleges. For the infrastructural improvement of this college RDC had played a great role.[32] Their second college was started in Chelannur, near Kozhikode in 1968. In the establishment of this college R. Sankar took special interest. An efficient RDC has also been working for this college since its establishment. This college is known as S. N. Guru College and it was great help to the people of this remote area in higher education. R. Sankar Memorial SNDP college in Koyilandy is the only college directly under the administration of SNDP yogam in Malabar.

Palakkad is an important centre of Ezhava community in Malabar. Their main educational institutions in the district are concentrated in Shornur.[33] Some leaders of SNDP in Shornur exhibited great courage to start a college for the community in this educationally backward area. C. Narayanan Waidyar, P. K. Gopalakrishnan and A. A. Jnanadevan were in the forefront of the community to begin a college. They decided to start a college under M. P. Muthedan and for this purpose they secured eight acres of land of Sree Narayana Seva Sangam. Thus, in 1981 the famous M.P.M.M.S.N. Trust College came into existence in Shornur.

Table 4.6 : List of Schools and Colleges under S.N. Trust and Yogam in Malabar

Districts	*Schools*	*Colleges*
Palakkad	3	3
Malappuram	–	1
Kozhikode	9	2
Kannur	3	1
Wayanad	9	1
Kasargode	3	1
Total	**27**	**9**

Source: Sree Narayana Directory 2009 (Kerala Kaumadi), Thiruvananthapuram, 2009, p.761.

Colleges of Nair Service Society

The attention of NSS in the advancement of higher education in Malabar was not effective like Travancore and Kochi. Out of the fifteen arts and science colleges run by NSS managements in Kerala, five colleges are situated in Malabar. Sree Vysa NSS College Vadkkancherry and other NSS Colleges Ottapalam, Nemmara, Manjeri and Mattannur are the colleges in Malabar. For the administration of the college NSS College Central Committee was formed and the administrative charge of affiliated colleges is held by convenor of this committee.[34]

NSS College, Ottapalam is an important college in Malabar with 12 degree courses and four post-graduate courses. In NSS college at Nemmara there are 11 degree courses and two post-graduate courses. These two colleges are the prominent colleges of NSS in Malabar. In NSS College, Manjeri and NSS College, Mattannur there are eight degree courses and two post-graduate courses; and nine degree courses and one post-graduate course respectively.

Government Colleges

The intervention of the government in the higher education sector of Malabar was very late compared to the private initiative in this sphere. The Calicut district had to wait till 1958 to have her first arts and science college at Madappally near Vadakara. In the academic year of 1960-61 there were 317 students on the rolls studying Pre-University, BA and B.Sc degree courses, in the college.

Table 4.7 : Number of Students in Govt. and Aided Colleges in Kerala: 1969 and 2007

	1969	*2007*		
Districts	*Total*	*Govt.*	*Aided*	*Total*
Thiruvananthapuram	18878	7880	15882	23762
Kollam	20395	262	16925	17187
Pathanamthitta	-	-	7816	7816
Alappuzha	14376	-	13768	13768
Kottayam	24483	1040	21055	22095
Idukki	-	631	3136	3767
Ernakulam	19708	3014	22225	25239
Trissur	14473	1802	17784	19586
Palghat	7058	4238	8268	12506
Malappuram	-	1757	8721	10478
Kozhikode	10837	4628	9514	14142
Wayanad	-	949	2235	3184
Cannanore	9553	2301	8049	10350
Kasargode		1751	1514	3265
Total	**139761**	**30253**	**156959**	**187212**

Source: Statistics for Planning 2009, DES, Thiruvananthapuram, 2009, p. 610.

Self-Financing Colleges

Alakkode, one of the early centres of migration had no chance for higher education after 60 years of migration. This vacuum could be filled by the migrants only in 2003. Under the Alakkode parish an arts and science college was established in 2003. It was Mary Mata Arts and Science College, Alakkode. B.Sc. Physics, Chemisrty, B.Com with computer application and English literature are the courses offered in this college.[35] For the starting of the college, trust was registered by the people of the parish including the vicar and assistant vicar of the parish and vicar general of the diocese. Under this trust a college advisory committee and finance committee was formed for the college. This made the recognition of the college very easy. By 2005-06, a permanent building for the college was constructed.

Agriculture College

Since the predominant occupation of the people in the rural area is agriculture the government established a separate university for study and research in agriculture. Kerala Agricultural University was established in 1971 in Trissur and several Agriculture, Veterinary, Horticulture, Fisharies and Forestry Colleges were started in different parts of the state. Such colleges were started in several parts of Malabar also. College of Agriculture at Padannakkad (Kasargode); College of Veterinary and Animal Sciences, Pookod (Wayanad); Kelappaji College of Agricultural Engineering and Technology, Tavanur (Malappuram) are chief colleges of this category in Malabar.

The School of Distance Education

The two universities in Malabar viz. Calicut University and Kannur University have their own distance education wings offering undergraduate (U.G.) and postgraduate (P.G.) courses. Calicut university established its distance education (DE) programme in 1981, followed by Kannur University in 2002.[36] Enrolmentwise, the School of Distance Education of Calicut University is the biggest in Kerala. According to the estimate 59.94 per cent of the distance education students of Kerala study through Calicut University in Malabar.[37] The working of distance education has been a great help to candidates who are not able to attend regular colleges due to various reasons. The students who are unable to get admission in regular colleges have resorted to distance education. The employed persons also opt conveniently for distance education without disturbing their permanent employment. Their chief aim was promotion in the service on the basis of additional qualification.

The students can study from their houses because directorate of distance education will provide printed study materials according to the syllabus of the university. The study materials prepared by the subject experts in each discipline are of high quality and suitable to get good score in the examination. This facility was not provided to private registration candidates of the university. Another significant advantage of this stream is that a ten days of contact classes are given to students in different parts of the state each year and it is free to students who registered in the distance education course. The registration fees and course fees of this stream are low and are affordable to even poor students of the society. Chiefly U.G. and P.G. courses in commerce, humanities and languages are offered in this stream. B.Com and M. Com; Economics, Sociology, History, Political Science, Malayalam, English and so on are the popular branches in the distance education mode. Thousands of students are making use of this facility of the universities. The School of Distance Education of Kannur University is offering nine U.G. Courses and four P.G. courses.

Table 4.8 : Enrollment of Distance Education (DE) Students in Kerala 2000

	Total DE Students	*percentage of Total DE Students*	*Total Students in Higher Edu.*	*percentage of DE Students in Higher Edu.*
Calicut University	24429	59.94	81622	29.92
Kerala University	4940	12.13	94757	5.2
M. G. University	2689	6.59	89262	3.01
IGNOU (Kochi Regional Centre)	8697	21.34	-	-
Total	40755	100		

Source: C. Krishnan, 'Distance Higher Education in Kerala-A Students' Assessment' in K. N. Nair and P. R. Gopinathan Nair (ed.) *Higher Education in Kerala: Micro Level Perspectives*, New Delhi, 2008, p.131.

Parallel Educational Institution in Malabar

The lack of regular educational institutions in the higher education sector led to the beginning of parallel colleges in Malabar. Before the origin of parallel colleges theses institutions were in the form of tutorials. The tutorials colleges had provided part time tuition to school and college going students. Earlier it was in the form of home tuition. The students generally sought tuition in tough subjects like Mathematics, English and Science. Their beginning was very humble. An educated but unemployed person usually provided tuition to the students. Later in the course of time the number of students increased and it became a permanent set up. When the number of pupil increased the centre of tuition was shifted from the residence of the teacher to a convenient place. Generally the new place was a building in the town and new teachers were appointed due to increase of the number of students. These institutions mainly worked in the morning and evening time i.e. before the beginning of the class and after the class. The tuition in these centres supplemented to the lessons they were taught in the regular classes. These institutions mainly offered courses in humanities and commerce streams because the science subjects needed high investment in the form of laboratory and other equipments. Though the first parallel institution was established in Kerala in 1934 these institutions came to be popular by1970's.[38]

Table 4.9 : District-wise List of Parallel and Tutorial Colleges in Kerala: 1989

	Parallel Colleges	*Tutorial Colleges*	*Parallel cum-Colleges*	*Total*
Thiruvananthapuram	22	475	217	714
Kollam	21	484	146	651
Pathanamthitta	12	165	66	273
Alappuzha	28	375	101	504
Kottayam	20	219	108	347
Idukki	9	26	85	120
Ernakulam	35	246	94	375

Trissur	67	257	85	409
Palghat	24	161	67	252
Malappuram	17	155	56	228
Kozhikode	38	198	113	349
Wayanad	6	20	25	51
Cannanore	25	112	131	268
Kasargode	7	29	24	60
Total	**331**	**2952**	**1318**	**4601**

Source: Report of the Survey on Parallel and Tutorial Colleges in Kerala 1989, DES, Thiruvananthapuram, 1990, p. 5.

In 1970's many of these tutorial colleges became parallel educational institutions offering regular classes of subjects in private registration. The Indian universities allowed students for the private registration for courses in different disciplines as per the Indian Education Commission Report of 1966.[39] The tutorial colleges arranged regular classes for the students who registered under the private and correspondence schemes of the university. Gradually these tuition centres attained the form of parallel colleges. The growth of parallel colleges was very fast because of the lack of adequate government or aided college in Kerala. In these colleges the students had to pay monthly fees and the running expenses including the salary of the teachers. Some successful institutions in a district opened the branches of their institutions in other parts of the district and even outside the district in a short period of time. Mercy College in Vadakara became an educational agency in Malabar with several institutions in different parts of Malabar. In many areas these private institutions engaged in tough competition between each other to seize the students. These institutions set apart a sizeable amount of money for the advertisement in their region to get students. The reason for the rapid and widespread increase in the demand for education in both school and higher education levels led to the growth of parallel educational institutions in Kerala. The parallel educational institutions played a very important role in the educational development of Malabar.

In Malabar, University of Calicut started private registration scheme in 1976.[40] The students chiefly joined in pre-degree courses, Bachelor of Arts, Bachelor of Commerce and Post Graduation in humanities and commerce.[41] Private individuals as well as co-operative agencies established such institutions all over Malabar offering various course to the students. The courses of other universities like Madras University, Annamalai University, S. V. University (Tirupathi), Madurai Kamaraj University etc. were also offered in these parallel institutions because the official procedures and syllabus in these institutions are much easier than the universities in Kerala. The students who privately registered their name for university degrees studied in parallel institutions. The functioning of these institutions was a great help to the students because the college authorities took all the responsibility to overcome the procedures in the university and arrange the centres of exam for their students in the districts. The enrolment of girls was high in the parallel institutions of Kerala. Most of the institutions conducted parallel and tutorial courses simultaneously and they were Tutorial cum 'Parallel Colleges'.

Table 4.10 : District-wise List of Parallel Students in Various Courses 1989

Districts	*Pre-Dergee*	*B.A.*	*B. Com.*	*M.A.*	*M.Com.*	*B.Sc. /M.Sc.*
Thiruvananthapuram	4867	2690	2647	666	592	391
Kollam	4653	2298	1882	1032	367	166
Pathanamthitta	3923	433	1143	249	173	38
Alappuzha	4613	440	1351	263	109	17
Kottayam	4086	1092	1852	803	273	562
Idukki	2856	1447	1173	249	170	182
Ernakulam	8936	1123	4243	348	218	167
Trissur	9305	5241	5656	832	270	502
Palghat	4256	1039	1606	69	63	417
Malappuram	3086	1740	1398	4	35	192
Kozhikode	4183	4250	2602	258	203	426
Wayanad	1012	710	469	5	0	0
Cannanore	5170	4923	2304	444	177	541
Kasargode	1105	1159	482	111	22	46
Total	**62051**	**28585**	**28808**	**5333**	**2672**	**3647**

Source: *Report of the Survey on Parallel and Tutorial Colleges in Kerala 1989*, DES, Thiruvananthapuram, 1990, p.5

The number of students was very high for the pre-degree courses in the parallel colleges of Malabar. The colleges offered 'Third' and 'Fourth' group, respectively humanities and commerce to the students of the above colleges. Besides a parallel college had provided B.Com., B.A. in various subjects and postgraduation (M.A. and M Com.) in selected subjects. The average number of students in the parallel colleges of Malabar was 472, but the number was high in Trivandrum and Cochin.[42] According to an estimate of 1996 the number of parallel educational institutions in Kerala was 4601. Of these 741 institutions were in Thiruvananthapuram district which was the highest in Kerala. Wayanad district has got only 51 parallel colleges which was the lowest in the state. All together 8,39,804 students were studied in these colleges in Kerala.

Moosad Brothers (M.B.) colleges was the first parallel educational institution in Kozhikode. National College (Kozhikode), Vishwabharathi College (Nadakkavu), Mercy College (Vatakara), Reshmi College (Koduvally), Calicut College (Koduvally) and Arts College (Vatakara) are the top institutions of this category in Kozhikode. More than 1000 students study in many of these institutions. The number of higher education institutions in the private sector of Malabar outnumbered the government institutions. Several educational agencies especially run by the religious entities opened their own institutions in higher education sector.

The lacuna in higher education institutions in Wayanad district was filled by the parallel educational institutions to a certain extent. Most of these institutions were started in the form of small tuition centres in the district by the migrants and later it was developed into major institutions. Some of them were registered under Co-operative Societies Act and became major private institutions in the district. Newmans's College, Mananthavady, Co-operative College, Mananthavady, Co-operative College, Sulthan Bathery, Co-operative College, Pulpally, Kumar College, Meenangadi and Malabar College, Kalpetta are some of the major parallel educational institutions in Wayanad.[43] All these institutions offer

U.G. and P.G. degrees of universities inside and outside the state in open stream.

Though Mananthavady was a major centre of migration in Wayanad, the students of this area had no facility for higher education for a very long time. This situation underwent a change when a private college was established in 1971 known as Newman's college in Mananthavady. This college was started by Mr Cherian a migrant from Travancore.[44] He looked after the college till 1979. Later under the inspiration of Fr. George Kazhikkachalil, Cherian the founder of the college gave it to the diocese of Mananthavady. This institution was a milestone in the educational history of Wayanad. Today this college offers two Post Graduate degree and three Under Graduate degrees for the students.

In Jayamatha College, Palakkad was a parallel college for women started in 1979. One of the famous women Christian religious congregations called Congregation of Mother of Carmel (CMC) established this college for women. The aim of this college was to fill gap between the facilities and requirements for higher education among the girl students in Palakkad. The number of students in 2005-06 academic year were 1550, which was higher than that in any other colleges of Palakkad. Some of the other famous parallel educational institutions run by Christian congregations in Palakkad are Mariyan College, Koduvayur (1978), Jyothi College, Mannarkkad (1989) and Sacred Heart College, Shornur (1978).

Parallel Colleges under MES

When the government started direct payment in the colleges in 1973 onwards the attitude of the government in permitting the new aided college was negative. But the real situation was that there was great gap between the demand and supply in the field of higher education. When the demand for new colleges from different parts of the state increased prominent management started parallel colleges in various areas of Malabar. As the long standing demand of MES for a women's college in Kozhikode was neglected by the government the Ladies Wing of MES started a Women's College in Kozhikode under the leadership of Fathima Ghafoor, the president of All India Muslim Educational Society in 1975. For the building only they spend rupees seven lakh apart from land. The college conducted Pre-Degree, Degree and PG courses in different subjects and PG Diploma courses including Diploma in Home Science. It was a great attraction of students to this college. In 1987, the number of students increased to 1300 from 150 in 1975. MES greatly encouraged and supported its district and taluk committees for beginning of Parallel colleges in Malabar. The main MES Parallel Colleges of Malabar are situated in Koyilandy, Nilambur, Vandoor, Trissur, Perinthalmanna, Valancherry, Kalpetta and Bathery.

The government and people of Malabar neglected higher education in the earlier period. When the school education spread among the common people extensively people realised the need for higher education. The limited number of colleges were not able to give enough facilities for students in the Malabar region. But the intervention of private agencies like MES, Christian institutions, SNDP, NSS and individual trusts established several colleges in different parts of Malabar. This filled the vacuum in higher education to a great extent. A few government colleges also played their own part in providing higher education but they were not able to give new courses and quality education to the students. But parallel colleges were the main resort to the students of rural areas for their higher education. The students joined for degree and postgraduate courses in private stream offered by different universities inside and outside the country. Moreover, the students of Malabar also depended largely on distance education programme of Calicut and Kannur universities. In short, when the government failed to provide higher education to the people of Malabar, the private agencies played their part very commendably.

References

1. University of Madras was founded in 1857 as per direction of Wood's Depatch of 1854.

2. William Logan, *Malabar Manual* Vol.1, New Delhi, p. 106.
3. It was established by Sri Chitra Tirunal Balarama Varma under the leadership of C. P. Ramaswamy Ayyar. For additional details see K. Shivasankaran Nair, *Ananthapuri Noottandukalilude*, Kottayam, 2004, pp. 130-131.
4. Later Mahatma Gandhi University at Kottayam and Kannur University at Kannur were started for the educational development of Kerala.
5. The Rate Schools in the Madras Presidency were depended on educational 'rate' levied by the Local Government for its expense. The Rate system was abolished in Malabar when Local Fund Act was implemented in 1871. All the Rate Schools were taken over by the Local Fund Board.
6. *Keralam Erupatham Noottandu*, (special supplement of Malayam Weekly), Thiruvananthapuram, p.139.
7. Kothari Commission Report cited in Raghavan, J. Veera, (ed.) *Higher Education in the Eighties: Opportunities and Objectives*, New Delhi, 1985, p. 248.
8. Under this parent body several other institutions are functioning for the educational advancement of the Muslim community. They are Farook Training College (1961), Farook Higher Secondary School (1954), Al-Farook English Medium Residential School (1991), Al-Farook Educational Centre (1991) and Farook Institution of Management Studies. All these institutions are functioning in the same campus of Farook College in Calicut.
9. *67th Session Souvenir*, Indian History Congress, Farook College, Calicut, 2007, p. 57.
10. They provided the name of Sir Syed Ahamed Khan (leader of All India Muslim League and freedom figher), who made tremendous contribution to the educational development of the Muslims.
11. It was the first indigenous Christian religious congregation founded in 1831 by Blessed Kuriakose Elias Chavara and two others.
12. Thomas Mathew Pallivathukkal from Mananthavady in Wayanad was the first student of this college. For more details refer *Yobel*, Golden Jubilee Souvenir, St. Joseph's College, Devagiri, Kozhikode, 2006, pp. 31-32.
13. The college is registered under the Apostolic Carmel Education Society in 1957 (Calicut). The Managing Governing Body includes the Provincial Superior, Educational Secretary, the Principal, the Local Manager, a representative of the management and a religious staff nominated by the provincial superior.
14. The Travancore University was started in 1937 and later it was rechristened University of Kerala in 1957. Till the formation of the

University of Calicut in 1968 the entire Kerala region was under the jurisdiction of University of Kerala. When the University of Calicut was formed the Malabar region came under this university.

15. *Fr. Mathai Nooranal Smaranika 2003*, St. Mary's Orthodox Cathedral, Sulthan Bathery, 2003, p.78.

16. Now it has became a college with four Masters degree course and eleven Under Graduate courses.

17. The idea of a college in Pulpally was appeared in the discussions on a *Devasvam* land issue. When a group of people claimed over a plot of 25 acres of land near to the Seetha Devi temple at Pulpally, in the all party meeting the *Devasvam* authorities and leaders of political parties agreed on the formation of a college in Pulpally. Information given by V. N. Lakshmanan, D. C. C. Secretary, Wayanad. He was the former member of Pazhassi Raja Education Society, Pulpally.

18. *Directory 2007-2008*, Archeparchy of Kottayam, 2008, p. 271.

19. The third ministry of Kerala (1967-1970) had two chief ministers viz. EMS Namboodiripad (1967-69) and C. Achutha Menon (1969-1970). Under EMS Namboodiripad's tenure minister of education C. H. Muhammad Koya took great effort in the beginning of University of Calicut. For more details see *Election Guide 2006,* Malayala Manorama, Kottayam, 2006, p. 50.

20. It was originally established by the name 'Malabar University' in 1995 by an Ordinance of the Governor of Kerala.

21. But the state average of the Muslim growth of population was 37 per cent. For more information see *Census of India 1981*, Final Population Totals-Kerala, 1982, p. 29.

22. P. K. Abdul Gafoor expressed this uneasiness in a public meeting in Kozhikode. Quoted in *M E S Charithram 1964-94,* Calicut, 1994, p. 34.

23. *Dr. Gafoor Sahib Smaranika*, MES Kerala, Calicut, 1985, p. 45.

24. Dr P.K. Abdul Ghafoor was born in at Kodungallur on 25 December 1929. He graduated from Aligarh Muslim University and he passed M.B.B.S. from Trivandrum Medical College in the first batch. He attained M.R.C.P. from Edinburgh with specialisation in Neurology in 1962, probably the first Muslim who passed M.R.C.P. in South India. He was appointed as Assistant Professor in Calicut Medical College in 1963 and continued in government service till his resignation from the post of Associate Professor in 1972 to devote more time to the cause of Muslim education and social work. In 1973, he was elected as the president of All India Muslim Education Society (AIMES). He died in 1984. For additional information regarding Dr P.K. Abdul Ghafoor see *Voice of Islam,* 7, 33 (1984), pp. 32-34.

25. In 1964-65 MES provided scholarship to 98 students. They were medical

students -12, engineering college students 21, polytechnic students-26, BEd. Students-3, TTC students-1 and other 35 students were from Pre-Degree, Degree and Post Graduation courses. MES Charithram 1964-94, Calicut, 1994, p. 64.

26. *Muslim Educational Society Souviner 1967*, Calicut, 1967, p. 11.
27. *Ibid.*, p. 13.
28. The name of this college changed in 1984 as 'Dr. Ghafoor Memorial MES Mampad College' in memory Dr. P. K. Abdul Ghafoor, the first president of MES who saved this institution at the time a crisis in 1969.
29. He served as the General Secretary of the SNDP Yogam from 1944-1954 and 1956-57. He served as the Chief Minister of Kerala from 1964-66.
30. When he was the General Secretary of SNDP Yogam he accumulated rupees one lakh in a single day for starting educational institutions.
31. *Sree Narayana Directory 2009* (Kerala Kaumadi), Thiruvananthapuram, 2009, p.760.
32. The former RDC members of S. N. College, Kannur Kaliyath Damodaran and Dr. T. P. Balakrishnan greatly contributed for the infrastructural development of the college.
33. In Palakkad alone SNDP Yogam have nine unions and 419 Shakas which is highest among the districts of Malabar. For more information see *Sree Narayana Directory 2009* (Kerala Kaumadi), Thiruvananthapuram, 2009, p.771.
34. NSS College Central Committee is ten member committee for the administration of the colleges under NSS management. The President, General Secretary, Treasurer and Assistant Secretary of NSS are the ex-officio members of this committee.
35. *Suvarna Jubilee Smaranika 1995-2005*, St. Mary's Forane Church, Alakkode, 2005, p. 151.
36. The first correspondence course in Kerala was started in 1977 by Kerala University.
37. C. Krishnan, 'Distance Higher Education in Kerala-A Students' Assessment' in K. N. Nair and P. R. Gopinathan Nair (ed.) *Higher Education in Kerala: Micro Level Perspectives*, New Delhi, 2008, p.131.
39. The Indian Education Commission under Dr. D. S. Kothari was appointed in 1964. He suggested correspondence courses, evening colleges and private registration in the universities in India.
40. In Kerala private registration was first started in 1971 by Kerala University. In 1975-76 only 22 universities in India offered correspondence courses in India. For more information see Nair, P. R. Gopinathan and D. Ajith, *Parallel Colleges in Kerala: A Case Study of their Structure in Terms of*

Enrollment Costs and Employment (Working Paper No. 156), Centre for Development Studies (CDS), Trivandrum, 1983, pp. 6-8.

41. University of Calicut came into existence in 1968. Since its inception the university provided private registration for the students. This was a reason for the rapid spread of parallel educational institutions in Malabar.
42. In Trivandrum and Cochin the average number of student was 1078 and 672 respectively in 1981-82. See Nair, P. R. Gopinathan and D. Ajith, *Parallel Colleges in Kerala: A Case Study of their Structure in Terms of Enrollment Costs and Employment* (Working Paper No. 156), Centre for Development Studies (CDS), Trivandrum, 1983. p. 16.
43. In the absence of government and aided colleges several private and parallel institutions were established in Wayanad. Sandeepani college, started in 1976 was the only institution in Pulpally that offered U.G. and P.G. degree courses.
44. *Cascade*, Annual Magazine, Newman's College, Mananthavady, 2008, p. 13.

5
Teacher Training Education

The teacher training in Kerala kept pace with other fields of education only by the beginning of the twentieth =1 century when new educational institutions began to crop up in the princely state of Kerala and Malabar under Madras Presidency. Though educational institutions in modern line started appearing in the second half of the nineteenth century the appointment of professionally trained teachers in the primary or secondary level was not a matter of concern. The general attitude of the society was that anybody slightly superior in qualification to the pupils was competent enough to teach.[1] Especially in the vernacular schools established by individual and institutional entities the professionally trained teachers were not available for the appointment. The lack of professionally trained teachers in educational institutions of Travancore, Cochin and Malabar was a serious handicap in the education sector of Kerala. But the situation began to change only after the second half of the twentieth =1 century.

The condition of Madras Presidency in which Malabar formed a district and the princely states of Travancore and Cochin did not realise the need of teacher education though training was most vital for the sound system of education. The lack of modern subjects in teaching and instruction in religious and traditional subjects did not need training. But the situation began to change when the British introduced English education in the schools. The greatest problem faced by the schools was the shortage of qualified teachers.[2] The teachers who used English as the medium of instruction and teaching of non-religious subjects needed special training in teaching profession. The British established teacher training schools in India in the middle of the nineteenth century.

Early Training Institutions

The British teacher training schools were called Normal Schools. The first Normal School in South India was established in Madras in 1856. The Wood's Despatch of 1854, stressed the need for the appointment of qualified teachers in the schools and maintain proper standard of teaching. The British government established the first Normal School in Kerala at Kannur in 1861. The British wanted trained teachers for English education in Malabar. A few seats in this school were reserved for students of Travancore on condition that the later would give a sum for its maintenance. Travancore had to wait till 1866-67 for the beginning of the first Normal School. In the beginning of Normal School, only 25 seats were sanctioned and stipends were given to the students. Admission was opened to all teachers for the one year duration course. For the teachers of elementary schools separate training was given for English schools and vernacular schools.[3]

Basic Training Schools

Basic Training Schools were established in colonial period for the training of teachers. Those who passed Higher Elementary (III Form) joined the Basic Training Schools. After one year's course they passed Training School Leaving Certificate (TSLC) examination. Secondary and Elementary grades of examination were held in Malabar and Travancore area. Most of the training schools were attached to Secondary schools in Malabar.[4] In many areas separate training schools for boys and girls were established. Government Basic Training School for Men, Anakkara and Government Basic Training School for Women, Palakkad were examples of separate institutions. Sevamandir Basic Training School at Ramanattukara was example of private training school. Koduvayur, Tirur, Malappuram, Vadakara, Palayad and Maipady are the centres of training schools in Malabar.

In the course of time government streamlined the teacher training in the state. The training period in the Basic training schools was increased to two years and the name of the course was changed to Teacher Training Certificate (TTC). According to the estimate of the government the total number of Basic Training Schools in Kerala in 1972-73 was 104. Out of this total number, 31 of them were government schools and 73 schools were private aided schools.[5] In the government Basic Training Schools in service courses were conducted for the untrained teachers in the schools. The number of students in the Basic Training Schools in 1961-62 was 7035 and it increased to 14526 in 1966-67.

Table 5.1 : Educational District-wise Basic Training Schools 1972-73

Educational Districts	*Govt.*	*Aided*	*Total*
Neyyattinkara	1	2	3
Thiruvananthapuram	1	2	3
Attingal	1	2	3
Quilon	1	4	5
Kottarakkara	1	5	6
Pattanamthitta	0	4	4
Alapuzha	1	3	4
Mavelikkara	2	5	7
Thiruvalla	1	6	7
Kottayam	2	5	7
Palai	1	3	4
Kanjirapally	0	2	2
Ernakulam	2	4	6
Muvattupuzha	1	3	4
Aluva	1	5	6
Irijalakkuda	1	4	5
Trissur	2	1	3
Chavakkad	0	2	2
Palakkad	2	2	4
Ottapalam	1	2	3

Malappuram	1	1	2
Tirur	1	2	3
Kozhikode	2	2	4
Vadakara	1	0	1
Thalassery	1	1	2
Kannur	2	0	2
Kasargode	1	1	2
Total	**31**	**73**	**104**

Source: Kerala Educational Statistics 1972-73, Directorate of Public Instruction, 1973, p.19.

Teacher Training Institutes

With the introduction of the universalisation of elementary education there was a great need for primary teachers in Kerala. Trained teachers were very essential in the lower primary education sector where the pupils up to fourth standard studied. For the teaching in lower primary schools the teachers were trained in the Teacher Training Institutes. In these institutes students complete two-year TTC courses.

Table 5.2 Teacher Training Institutes in Malabar 1986-87

District	*Government*	*Pvt. Aided*	*Total*	*No. of Students*
Palakkad	3	4	7	569
Malappuram	2	3	5	382
Kozhikode	3	2	5	402
Wayanad	-	1	1	80
Kannur	3	1	4	305
Kasargode	1	1	2	201
Total	**12**	**12**	**24**	**1939**

Source: Educational Statistics 1987, Dept. of Education, Trivandrum, 1987, p. 50.

As mentioned earlier one of the problems faced by the newly opened schools in Malabar was the scarcity of trained school teachers. Most of the teachers who served in Malabar were brought from Travancore with great strain.[6] The students of Malabar who wanted to pursue career of teaching at that time had to go either to Palakkad or Thissur for teacher training.[7] To solve this crisis Fr. George Kazhikkachalil took initiative for the starting of a training institute in Wayanad.[8] He was successful in getting permission from the government to open a training institute and thus, in 1963 St. Joseph's Teacher Training Institute was established at Mananthavady. At the beginning there were only two teachers and 26 teacher trainees and later it became a prestigious institution of Malabar. This was the first Teacher Training Institute started by the migrant community in Malabar.

Teacher Training in Post-Colonial Malabar (1947-2006)

As a part of the policy of increasing educational facilities in the districts by Madras state, Malabar needed new training schools. To solve the problem of scarcity of teachers in Malabar new Basic Training Schools were started in different parts of Malabar. Government started a new Basic Training School at Palakkad in 1947 and another such institution in Vadakara in 1949.[9] The government Basic Training School at Palayad was a famous teacher training centre of North Malabar.

The teachers of secondary school education were trained in training colleges. The teacher training colleges offered L.T. (Licentiate in Teaching) degree to the students. At first, very few students after their graduation went to the Teacher's Training College at Saidapet in Madras.[10] Later a training college was started at Trivandrum in 1911. This was the only training college in Kerala till the establishment of another college in Trissur in 1945. The number of seats for B. T. degree in Travancore was 120 in the year 1948.[11] The report of the Travancore Education Reform Committee gave detailed recommendations of teacher training in Travancore. By the integration of Travancore and Cochin the number of available seats in Travancore increased to 145. The first training college in Malabar was the Govt. Training College at Calicut founded in 1950.

After the integration of Travancore-Cochin and Malabar in 1956 the educational system of Kerala got a uniform pattern. By 1953, private managements also started training colleges in Travancore. Mount Carmal Training College, Kottayam (1953); N. S. S. Training College, Chenganassery (1954); and Mar Theophilus Training College, Thiruvananthapuram were the early training institutions of private management in Kerala. In tune with the increase of secondary schools in Kerala, government sanctioned six training colleges in 1957 and out of six colleges five institutions were sanctioned to private entities. In 1960, B.T. course had given place to BEd. Course of modern line.

Government College of Teacher Education, Kozhikode

The Madras Government shifted the only Government Training College in Malabar, which was situated in Palakkad as a part of Government Victoria College to Calicut in 1951. The college started its functioning in 1951 in the building of the Government School of Commerce built in 1910 when R.B. Wood was the Collector of Malabar.[12] The aim of the college was to impart teacher training in Secondary level to the teachers of Malabar.[13] At that time it was a recognised training college under the University of Madras. Following the reorganisation of state this institution came under University of Kerala for B.T. course.

Table 5.3 : Students of Kozhikode Training College in 1951-1956 Batch

Year	*Hindu*	*Christian*	*Muslim*	*Total*
1950-51	76	5	3	84
1953-54	88	6	6	100
1955-56	84	6	10	100

Source: Admission Register 1951-56, Vol.1, Government Training College, pp. 1-55.

The students who passed B.A. and BSc. Degree courses from various parts of Malabar, Cochin and Travancore had obtained admission for B. T. courses in this institution in Kozhikode. In the early years more than 80 per cent of the students belonged to Hindu caste especially high castes like Brahmins and Nairs. Moreover, students of Tiyas and several other backward classes also studied in this college. The number of girls who pursued their courses in the early years were low in the college. In the first year out of 84 students admitted only 15 students were girls.[14] Government had provided separate hostel facilities for boys and girls in the city. This was the resort of the students of entire Malabar for teacher training. Now a days this institution gained 'A' grade status of NAAC, the only institution of this standard in Malabar.

The entire North Malabar was neglected in the arena of teacher education till 1957. Government Training College in Thalassery, the second institution in this category was started in 1957.[15]

Teacher Training Institutions in Malabar

When compared to the training facilities in Travancore, the number of colleges in Malabar was very few. N.S.S. Training College at Ottapalam was the first teacher training institution in Malabar in private sector started in 1960. It was a milestone in the history of teacher training in Malabar. The limited government facilities for teacher training in Malabar was a serious handicap of school education because majority of the teachers appointed in the school were untrained. The students aspiring to become trained teachers had to rely on other parts of the state or even outside the state for teacher training. The lack of trained teachers adversely affected the standards of teaching and learning in the schools. The NSS Training College had a very humble origin in with only 80 students in the campus of NSS K.P.T. High School. The great rush for students to college resulted in the increase of students intake to 150 in 1965. In 2000, the strength of students again increased to 300, which is the highest number of seats in a training college in the state.[16] The starting of M.Ed course in 1995 was a great achievement in the annals of education history of Malabar. The establishment of Farook Training College in

1961 at Farrok near Calicut was the first such institution of Muslim minorities in Malabar. It was a turning point in the educational advancement of Muslim community in Malabar.

University Teacher Education Centres

The candidates of Malabar had only very limited facilities for teacher training. Apart from very few B.Ed. Colleges the students of Malabar studied in the Regional Institute of Education, Mysore.[17] The students had to relay on the institutions outside Kerala for their teacher training. They went to the colleges not only in Karnataka, Tamil Nadu, Andhra Pradesh but also in Assam for having their B.Ed. course. The great scarcity of teachers due to the lack of training facilities to the graduate was serious problem in the state since the beginning of large number of schools and in 1980s and 1990s. After 1982 the university directly started University Teacher Education Centres in all the districts for teacher education. All the Universities in Kerala started University teacher Education Centres for more seats in B.Ed. It was popularly known as 'Sessional B.Ed.' The beginning of classes and time of examination of these centres were different from that of regular B.Ed. courses under the university. In the case of Malabar also this crisis was met by the Calicut University by establishing University Teacher Education Centres under the university. Eleven such centres were started since 1996 by the Calicut University. Kannur University began three centres in Kannur, Kasargode and Mananthavady. Earlier 50 B.Ed. Seats were allotted to each college and later the seats increased to 100. These colleges were run on the cost based system of the university by taking entire fees from the students. In practice, these institutions are the self-financing B.Ed. Colleges run by the university.

Each centre was under a Director appointed by the university and he may be a well experienced teacher in educational training. The teachers appointed in these colleges were on temporary basis and yearly extension was given to the teachers. Seats to each branch of B.Ed. were allotted on the basis of local demand of teachers. Social Science, Malayalam, Hindi, English, Sanskrit,

Arabic, Natural science, Physical Science, Maths, Commerce and Computer Science are the chief branches of B.Ed. One important drawback of these centres is the lack of enough infrastructural facilities in the teacher education centres. Most of these centres were started either in school building or rented buildings in the towns with no facilities for students. These centres also needed the approval of National Council of Teacher Education (NCTE) and there were several instances of loosing the approval of NCTE due to the lack of facilities. The University Teacher Education Centres under Calicut University are situated in Calicut, Vadakara, Kaniyambetta, Manjeri, Palakkad, Trissur, Sulthan Bathery, Balussery, Malappuram, Valappad and Nattika.

Self-financing Institutions

The scarcity of seats for B.Ed. course were very severe since 1998 at a time when the government began to delink Pre-Degree from the colleges and started the upgradation of High Schools into Higher Secondary School. The Degree like B.Ed. has been one of the mandatory qualifications for teachers in Higher Secondary Schools. In the year 2000 the delinking of Pre-Degree was completed and there was a great rush for B.Ed. courses and the students had to move to other states to acquire this qualification. Besides, requirement of M.Ed. Degree was accelerated while the government made M.Ed. equivalent to State Eligibility Test (SET). This test is another necessary qualification to become a teacher in Higher Secondary School and many candidates felt it very difficult to clear the SET examination.

To meet the urgent need of B.Ed. holders government sanctioned several self-financing teacher training colleges in Malabar. One of the early self-financing B.Ed. colleges in Malabar was Devaki Amma Memorial College of Teacher Education in Malappuram established in 1999. Then successive governments issued NOC to large number of institutions for the beginning of B.Ed. Courses. One important advantage of these institutions is high level of infrastructure provided to the students according to the specifications of NCTE. The growth of B.Ed. Colleges was very fast in Malabar within a decade 34 training colleges were established in different parts of Malabar. In each self-financing college government sanctioned 100 seats and out this 50 seats are filled by the management and rest of the seats are allotted to the students from the state merit list.

Table 5.4 : District and Category-wise Number of B.Ed. Colleges in Malabar : 2006

Districts	*Unaided*	*Aided*	*Govt.*	*UTEC*
Palghat	7	1		1
Malappuram	14			2
Kozhikode	8	1	1	3
Wayanad	3			3
Cannanore	1	2	1	1
Kasargode	1			1
Total	**34**	**4**	**2**	**11**

Source: Mathrubhoomi Uparipadanam Directory, Kozhikode, 2006, pp.173-174.

With the beginning of large number of B.Ed. Colleges there was a scarcity of M.Ed. seats in the state. M.Ed. is the essential qualification of teachers in B.Ed. Colleges. The students of Malabar had no opportunity for the degree of post-graduation in education (M.Ed.) till the Department of Education in the University campus started post-graduation in education. The intake capacity of M.Ed. course in the department was only 20 and another 20 seats were sanctioned for M.Ed. (Technology) on self-financing basis. As noted earlier in 1995-96 M.Ed. course was started in Farrok College and later in NSS Training College, Ottapalam. In both these institutions only 20 seats were sanctioned. Moreover, as research centre of the university department offered M.phil. and PhD. courses to the students.

One vital need of the educational progress is the availability of trained teachers. The lack of trained teachers was a major hindrance to the development of education in Malabar till 1980. When the number of secondary schools increased the shortage of teachers became very serious. The possibility of huge financial burden in opening new government training colleges forced the government to permit self-financing TTC and BEd. Colleges in the state. Besides, the universities set up self-financing University Teacher Education Centres for BEd. courses. The private institutions satisfied the need of the students in the case of teacher training courses in Malabar. In short, the government was forced to rely on private institutions in providing enough trained teachers for schools in Kerala.

References

1. For more details see M. Vijayakumari Amma, 'A Historical Perspective on the Teacher Education Programme in Kerala', in *Journal of Kerala Studies*, Vol.XXXII, 2005, p. 222.
2. Salim and Nair, *op. cit.*, p. 121.
3. The training institutes granted five certificates- High School Certificate and Middle School Certificate for English schools; and High School Certificate and Middle School Certificate and Primary School Certificate for Vernacular schools.
4. Lower Secondary and Secondary and Training School, Ottapalam; Government Secondary and Training School for Women, Kozhikode; Government Training School for Men, Kozhikode; Government Training School for Men, Kannur are some of the training institutions in Malabar.
5. *Kerala Educational Statistics 1972-73*, Directorate of Public Instruction, 1973, p.19.
6. Malabar was a part of Madras state before 1957 it was very difficult for the teachers to get government approval, whom trained in Travancore. For a detailed discussion on the difficulty of getting teachers to Malabar, see *Souvenir of Pulpally Immigration...*, Mullankolly, *op.cit.*, pp. 20-22.
7. Information given by P.A. Parameshwaran, former A. E. O. He served in the educational field of Wayanad for a long period from 1958 to 1982.
8. *Girideepam, Special issue*, *op.cit.*, p. 89.
9. From these institutions till 1951 government obtained 12 secondary trained teachers and 237 elementary trained teachers. For additional information see *Anjukollathe Nettangal-Malabar District*, Information and Publicity Department, Government of Madras, Madras, 1951, p. 39.
10. Vijayakumari Amma, *op. cit.*, p. 223.

11. The name of the degree changed from L. T. to Bachelor of Teaching (B.T.)

14. *Admission Register 1951-56*, Vol. 1, Government Training College, Kozhikode, 1951, pp. 1-9.

15. It was established as an Elementary School by Edward Brenan in 1862. *College Magazine 1993*, Government Training College, Thalassery, 1993, p. 4.

16. B.Ed course in six subjects viz Mathematics, Physical Science, Natural Science, Social Science, Malayalam and English are offering in this college.

17. Regional Institute of Education in Mysore was started in 1963 under NCERT to conduct better research and planning in the field of teacher education. The Government College of teacher Education in Kozhikode and Thalassery are the only two government BEd. Colleges in Malabar. The aided colleges are Farook Training College, Calicut; NSS Training College, Ottapalam; PKM College of Education, Madampam, Kannur and Keyi Sahib Training College, Karimbam, Taliparamba. For more information see *Uparipadanam*, Mathrubhoomi Directory, Kozhikode, 2006, p.

6
Development of Technical Education

The development of technical education was very late in Malabar. Engineering colleges, Polytechnics and Industrial Training Institutes had no place in the educational field of Malabar. But after 1960's Industrial units began to be established in Malabar especially in Palakkad and Kozhikode. Before that the professionally trained persons were not needed in Malabar for skilled jobs. The great demand for skilled labourers in Gulf countries since 1980's accelerated the need for new technical institutions in Kerala. Unemployment situation was very severe in Kerala in 1980's and 1990's because of the lack of industries in Kerala. People realised the fact that without proficiency in technical skills they could not tap the job opportunities in industrially developed parts of India and Gulf countries. Consequently the demand for new technical institutions like engineering colleges, polytechnics and Industrial Training Institutes became very high. The development of science and technology had increased the importance of technical education and the government started new engineering degree courses, diploma courses, postgraduate courses, certificate courses, junior technical school courses and industrial training courses in Kerala.

Polytechnic

Polytechnics in the state are common institutions that offer technical education to the students. The Board of Technical Education in Kerala controls the Polytechnics in Kerala. These institutions offer diploma courses in various branches of engineering. The most common diploma courses are in civil engineering, mechanical engineering, electrical engineering, electronics engineering, computer science, computer hardware maintenance, computer application and business management, automobile, electronics and telecommunication, textile technology, wood technology, instrumentation, tool and dye making, architecture and so on. Several Certificate courses in various branches in air conditioning, tool and dye making and so on are offered in these institutions.

The total number of polytechnics in Kerala was 13 during the period of 1964-65. The admission to seven government polytechnics and 85 per cent seats in six private polytechnics was done by a committee consisting of principals of polytechnics and the director of technical education. The total number of seats available for admission in polytechnics in Kerala was 1554 only but the applicants were as high as 6303.[1] This figure presents the urgent need for more technical institutions in Kerala. The admission to polytechnics was made strictly on the basis of marks obtained for Mathematics and General Science in SSLC and JTSLC. Government maintained 40 per cent reservation for backward and other special categories of students in polytechnics.

Out of the total number 25 Polytechnics in Kerala in 1986 only eight were in Malabar.[2] The first Polytechnic in Malabar was Kerala Government Polytechnic at West Hill in Calicut. It was established in 1946 with four diploma courses in Civil, Mechanical, Electrical and Chemical Engineering. After this institution the people of Malabar had to wait till 1958 for the second Polytechnic, Government Polytechnic at Thottada in Kannur. When the demand for skilled labour in small scale industries increased, the government commenced Polytechnics in Perinthalmanna (1961), Kozhikode (Women's 1963), Palaghat (1980) and Meenagadi (1984). A different institution established in Malabar in the technical field was Institute of Printing Technology in Shornur in 1967.

The government failed to fulfill the great need of technical education in Malabar because large number of unemployed youths were waiting for jobs inside and outside the country. To meet the urgent need of technical institutions the government sanctioned private polytechnics in Malabar since 1962. The private institutions were covered by the Grant-in-aid scheme of the government. The first private institution was accorded to Kerala Muslim Educational Association (KMEA) and they established Seethi Sahib Memorial Polytechnic at Tirur.[3] For the next private polytechnic government selected another educationally backward area, Hosdurg taluk of Kannur district. In1966, government sanctioned Swamy Nithyananda Polytecnic in Kanhangad with diploma course in Mechanical Engineering. When people demanded new courses government consented diploma in Automobile Engineering in 1967 and Civil Engineering in 1983. The courses in Polytechnics has became very attractive to students because a diploma holder can achieve B. Tech through Lateral Entry scheme.

Junior Technical Schools

The government started Junior Technical Schools (JTS) in the state to impart technical education and skill to the students in their early age. In 1964, there were 20 junior technical schools in Kerala with total intake capacity of 1200.[4] The admission to JTS was made on district basis. The admissions were made on the basis of marks obtained for the seventh standard examination. In the above year the number of JTSs in Malabar were only eight. They were established in Shornur, Manjeri, Cheruvathoor, Chittoor, Krishnapuram, Mattannur, Kannur and Calicut. In the estimate of 2007-08 the total number of Technical High Schools in the state increased to 44. Out of this 39 were government institutions and five were self-financing institutions. In the same period 6300 students studied in the Technical High Schools of the State.[5]

There were fifty private grant-in-aid technical schools which functioned in the state. Out of them thirty institutions prepared students for needle work examination in Kerala Government Technical Education (KGTE) and the remaining twenty institutions prepared students for KGTE in weaving. Admission to these institutions was made both from male and female candidates within the age group of 14-25 and from those who have passed III form or equivalent.[6]

Table 6.1 : Number of Technical Institutions in Malabar 1976

S. N.	*Districts*	*Polytechnics*		*Junior Technical Schools*	*Industrial Training Institutes*			*Total*
		Govt.	*Private*	*Govt.*	*Private*	*Govt.*	*Private*	
1.	Palakkad	1	-	2	-	1	-	4
2.	Malappuram	1	1	1	-	1	1	5
3.	Kozhikode	2	-	2	-	1	1	6
4.	Kannur	1	1	3	-	1	-	6

Source: Administration Report on Technical Education 1964-65: Kerala, Ernakulam, 1966, p.11.

Engineering Colleges

The first engineering college in South India was established at Guindy in Madras by the British. After independence the Government of India realised the need of technological advancement and rapid industrialisation. The government felt a great scarcity of technical personnal in the state and the help from the foreign countries was very meagure. To overcome this problem advanced central institutions like IIT (Indian Institute of Technology) were started in the country. The government established first IIT in the eastern region of India at Kharagpur in 1951. Madras became the first south Indian city to have an IIT in 1959. The first engineering college in Kerala was established in 1939 namely, College of Engineering Trivandrum (CET). Till the beginning of Govt. Engineering at Trissur in 1958 the former was the only engineering college in Kerala. The importance of science and technology prompted the government to start the renowned Cochin University for Science and Technology in 1971.

The different communities in Kerala showed great interest in the establishment of technical institutions in the state.[7] Half of the total seats in these institutions also was reserved for the concerned managements and the rest of the seats were merit seats of government. In the management quota of seats a portion of the seats was reserved for meritorious students of that particular community who owned the college. In 1964-65, the admission to all the seats in the government engineering colleges and 85 per cent of the seats in the private engineering colleges were made by the Department of Technical Education.[8] The total number of seats available in all engineering colleges and total number of candidates applied for admission in 1964 were 760 and 3612 respectively.[9] The admission to these colleges was made on the basis of marks obtained by the candidates in the Pre-University Examination for Mathematics, Physics and Chemistry. When more colleges were sanctioned by the government the admission of students to these colleges was a serious problem. For a merit based selection of students to the government seats All Kerala Common Entrance Examination was started by the government.

In Malabar N. S. S. Engineering College at Palakkad was the first institution in this category. NSS conceived the idea of an engineering college in Malabar to cater to the growing need for technically skilled people in Kerala. They identified land in Akathethara in Palakkad for this engineering college and started the first private management aided engineering college in 1960. The NSS Engineering College in Palakkad is the only engineering college of Nair Service Society in the state. The major engineering departments are Electricity and Electronics, Mechanical, Industrial, and Civil Engineering.

But the premier engineering educational institution in Malabar was the Regional Engineering College (REC) Calicut established by the central government in 1961. In the beginning civil engineering was given importance in the college but later electrical and mechanical engineering courses started in this college. In 1985-86 the college commenced new courses in Computer Science, Production and Management, Electronics and Communication and Architecture (5-year course). This college was the only resort for the people of Malabar who want to pursue post graduate course in engineering. Since the beginning of the college, post graduate courses were started in Structural Engineering, Refrigeration and Air Conditioning, Industrial Engineering and Instrumental and Control System. This institution has been a pride to the people of Malabar for decades. In 2003, the Government of India elevated this premier technical institution of Malabar into a deemed-to-be-university named National Institute of Technology.

North Malabar was completely deprived of engineering institutions till two decades ago. The government neglected the cry of the people for engineering institutions for four decades and this situation changed in 1986 when Government College of Engineering started at Kannur. The starting of Civil Engineering, Mechanical Engineering, Electronics and Communication Engineering and Electrical and Electronics Engineering were a great help to the students of North Malabar because these are the popular branches in engineering education. The growth of technical institutions was tremendous in the last two or three decades. In the case of Malabar there were only three engineering colleges in 1977 but its number increased to 18 in 2007. Besides Kannur University had five affiliated engineering colleges in Malabar.

After the beginning of several colleges and large number of schools the attention on MES turned to technical institutions. The cost of starting an engineering college was very high compared to an ordinary college, so there was a lack of engineering institutions in private sector in Malabar till the beginning of NSS engineering college in Palakkad in1960. Moreover, an engineering college needed the approval not only of the government of Kerala but also of All India Council for Technical Education (AICTE) in New Delhi. MES took the challenge of beginning an engineering college in Malabar and they secured 32 acres of land near Valancherry town in Malappuram district for engineering college.[10] After completing all the procedures MES Central Committee established the first engineering college under Muslim management in Malabar in 1994. This was the first engineering college which secured status in Kerala. In the first year itself college started B.Tech course in

Mechanical, Applied Electronics and Instrumentation, Computer Science, Electronics and Communication. Later B. Arch. and Civil Engineering were started in this college. Today over 2750 students undertake their undergraduate and postgraduate courses here, under the expertise of over 400 qualified faculty members and research guides.

Institute for Human Resource Development (IHRD)

This is an autonomous institution under government of Kerala started in 1987. Government conceived this idea when the society felt the scarcity of skilled manpower in Electronics and Information Technology sector. Since the government institutions were not adequate for the requirements in the industrial sector, government started technical institutions under IHRD. The vision of the government was that preparing of human resources is the first step to solve unemployment situation in state. The government established nine engineering colleges, seven model polytechnics, 27 applied science colleges under IHRD in the state. Recently government institutes like Lal Bahadur Shatri Institute (LBS Institute) run engineering colleges in the state. LBS College of Engineering in Kasargode established in 1993 was a prominent institution in Malabar under LBS Institute. This is the only college in Malabar selected by the Government of India for its Technical Education Quality Improvement Programme (TEQIP).[11] Cooperative Institute of Technology, Kozhikode is also an engineering institution in Malabar.

Private Self-financing Institutions

Huge investment in infrastructure development and high salary given to the teachers are the chief reasons for the gradual withdrawal of government from the service sector especially education. When compared with ordinary arts and science colleges the initial investment is very huge in the case of professional educational institutions like B.Ed. Colleges, engineering colleges and medical colleges. The year 2001 was the turning point in the history of self-financing education because the government decided to give no objection certificate (NOC) to all institutions which applied for new institution especially management, engineering and medical institutions.[12] When government sanctioned these institutions 50 per cent of the total seats was reserved for government quota and the management was allowed to the rest of the seats. Through this government expected one government college by sanctioning two self-financing colleges. In general the initial cost of a self-financing college was very high because the management had to keep the specifications of the high power councils of the central government. After getting NOC from the state government the B.Ed. colleges required the approval of National Council of Teacher Education (NCTE). Engineering colleges required the permission of All India Council for Technical Education (AICTE) and medical colleges had to get the approval of Medical Council of India (MCI). They used to inspect all the institutions thoroughly before giving approval to these institutions. Due to their strictness in inspection management incurred heavy expense for the construction and maintenance of teachers in self-financing institution.

Table 6.2 : District-wise and Management-wise Engineering Colleges in Kerala 2007

Districts	*Govt.*	*Aided*	*Unaided*	*Total*
Thiruvananthapuram	2	0	13	15
Kollam	0	1	8	9
Pathanamthitta	0	0	5	5
Alappuzha	0	0	3	3
Kottayam	1	0	6	7
Idukki	1	0	3	4
Ernakulam	0	1	12	13
Trissur	2	0	8	10
Palghat	1	1	1	3
Malappuram	1	0	3	4
Kozhikode	1	0	3	4
Wayanad	1	0	0	1
Cannanore	1	0	3	4
Kasargode	0	0	2	2
Total	**11**	**3**	**70**	**84**

Source: Mathrubhoomi Uparipadanam Directory, Kozhikode, 2006, pp.173-174.

One of the prominent charitable trusts in Malabar which works in the self-financing educational field is Kunhitharuvai Memorial Charitable Trust (KMCT) established in 1994. It was founded by Dr K. Moidu and registered as a public trust and managed by a board of trustees. The trust obtained KMCT College of Engineering in 2001 itself, a self-financing engineering college with six B. Tech courses. In the technical field KMCT started a self-financing Polytechnic College in 2004[13]. Another famous charitable association of Malabar was Association for the Welfare of Handicapped (AWH) for the betterment of handicapped people in the society. This association established AWH College of Engineering in 2001 in Kozhikode as fillip to the growth of engineering course in Malabar.

The beginning of Vimal Jyothi Engineering College at Chemperi in Kannur in 2002 was turning point in the development of technical education in the rural villages of the undeveloped northern Malabar. When the government neglected the rural areas of Malabar in technical education, the Arch-diocese of Thalassery took interest in the beginning of this unaided engineering college. The college secured recognition for 300 seats in different branches of engineering courses. They included engineering courses like Electronics and Communication, Computer Science, Electrical and Electronics, Applied Electronics and Instrumentation and Mechanical. Sree Narayana Guru College of Engineering and Technology at Payyanur in Kanuur was the another unaided engineering college under Kannur University.[14]

Among the unaided professional colleges in Kerala, highest number of colleges are engineering colleges. This is because of soaring need of engineering professional inside and outside the country due to economic growth. The students of Kerala especially Malabar suffered severe hardships due to the lack of engineering courses in the state. The financial burden restrained the government from opening engineering colleges in the state. When the demand from the people for new institutions of professional courses became strong, the government allowed private agencies to start unaided professional colleges. In tune with this decision large number of engineering colleges started in Kerala. The number of engineering seats increased from 6300 in 2000-01 to 26430 in 2007-08.

References

1. *Administration Report on Technical Education 1964-65: Kerala*, Ernakulam, 1966, p.7.
2. *Man Power Series 61: Kerala*, Department of Economics and Statistics, Thiruvananthapuram, 1988, pp.120-121.
3. This polytechnic was the first technical institution started by Muslim community in Malabar and very advantageous for the educationally backward Malappuram region. Diploma courses in Civil Engineering, Mechanical engineering, Electronic Engineering and Automobile Engineering were commenced in this institution.
4. *Administration Report on Technical Education 1964-65: Kerala*, Ernakulam, 1966, p.7.
5. *Statistical Review 2007*, State Planning Board, Thiruvananthapuram, 2007,p. 337.
6. *Administration Report..., Ibid.*, p. 8.
7. Three early private engineering colleges in Kerala were Thangal Kunju Musaliar Engineering College, Quilon, NSS Engineering College, Palakkad and Mar Athanasius College of Engineering, Kothamangalam.
8. The selection of candidates to the engineering colleges was made by a committee consisting of the principals of engineering colleges; chairman, Kerala State Electricity Board; chief engineer (General and Irrigation); Registrar, University of Kerala and the Director of Technical Education.
9. *Administration Report on Technical Education 1964-65*, Ernakulam, 1966, p. 6.
10. Thangal Kunju Musliar Engineering College at Kollam was the only engineering college in Kerala under Muslim management established in 1958.
11. The other institution in Malabar in this programme in National Institute of Technology (NIT). TEQIP is a special programme of Central Government to improve the quality of technical education by upgrading the standard of technical educational institutions. This programme was funded by World Bank and IDA. The other institutions selected from Kerala are College of Engineering, Thiruvananthapuram; S. C. T. College

of Engineering, Thiruvananthapuram; Model Engineering College, Kochi and College of Engineering, Chengannur.

12. Eleventh Ministry of Kerala led by United Democratic Front (UDF) under the chief ministership of A. K. Antony (2001-2004) sanctioned maximum number of self-financing institutions in Kerala.
13. It was approved by All India Council of Technical Education and Government of Kerala.
14. There was only one government engineering college under Kannur University. It was established in 1986.

7

Medical, Law and Management Education

In the growth of medical education in Malabar the participation of the government was less when compared with other parts of Kerala. Out of the five government medical colleges in Kerala the Malabar region had to be satisfied with only one in Calicut. It was for the people of six districts in Malabar. The other four medical colleges in Thiruvananthapuram, Kottayam, Alappuzha and Trissur catered to the needs of the people of other eight districts in Kerala. This injustice to the people of Malabar district is still continuing. In the case of Ayurveda medical colleges only one was allotted to Malabar and other two were given to Travancore.

Table 7.1 : Government Medical Institutions in Malabar 1951

Districts	*Hospital*	*P.H.C.*	*Dispensary*	*T. B. Clinic*	*Others*	*Total*
Palakkad	10	11	55	1	1	78
Malappuram	7	12	46	2	1	68
Kozhikode	9	15	47	1	-	68
Kannur	12	13	98	2	1	126
Total	**38**	**51**	**246**	**6**	**3**	**340**

Source: Statistics of Kerala 1957, Bureau of Economics and Statistics, Thiruvananthapuram, 1958, p.12.

The first civil hospital in Malabar was started in 1845 at Calicut. The government started hospitals in Kasargode (1873), Majeshwaram (1892) and Hosdurg (1892) other than several public health centres. The first mental hospital in Malabar was also set up in Puthiyara near Calicut in 1872. The beginning of Kozhikode Medical College in 1957 was a turning point in the history of medical education in Malabar.

Now a days Kozhikode Medical College offers 200 M.B.B.S. seats, 40 B.D.S. seats, 60 BSc. Nursing seats and 20 seats for pharmacy course besides a large number of Post Graduate courses in different branches of medicine. The students for MBBS and other courses for these medical colleges have been selecting through an entrance examination, consequently only a few seats are available for the students of Malabar. Moreover, among these seats a certain seats were reserved for students of all India merit, so the number of seats for MBBS courses are too limited to the students of Malabar. The students of Malabar were forced to secure MBBS and M D seats in Tamil Nadu, Karnataka and Andhra Pradesh and outside the county like Nepal and Russia. This situation was created by the government due to reluctance to sanction medical colleges in private sector. The heavy financial burden prevented the government to start new government medical colleges in the state.

When United Democratic Front (UDF) government under A.K. Antony came to power in 2002, due to the pressure from the people the government decided to sanction self-financing educational institutions for professional courses. In the successive years several self-financing medical colleges were established all over Kerala. Some of the Allopathic medical colleges are started in Malabar recently. MES Medical College at Perithalmanna was one the early self-financing medical colleges in Malabar. Karuna Medical College (Palakkad), KMCT Medical College (Kozhikode), Academy of Medical Sciences, Pariyaram and Kannur Medical College at Anjarakkandy are the unaided medical colleges in north Malabar. The seat sharing issues and fees structure in the merit seats and payment seats led to several legal battles between government and managements.[1]

Side by side with the growth Allopathy medicine the government encouraged alternative medicines also in Kerala.

The Govt. Ayurveda College in Kannur established in 1991 was the only government institution of this category in Malabar. This college offer not only BAMS course and but MD courses in *Roganidana* and *Kriyasareera*. But in this section also unaided institutions satisfied the needs of the students. P. S. Warrier Medical College in Kottakal, Santhigiri Ayurveda Medical College (Palakkad), Vishnu Ayurvedea College (Shornur) and KMCT Ayurveda College (Kozhikode) are unaided Ayurveda colleges in south Malabar. Parassinikadauvu Ayurveda Medical College was the only unaided Ayurveda Medical College under Kannur University in north Malabar. This college offer BAMS; B.Sc. Nursing (Ayurveda) and B. Pharm (Ayurveda) courses.

Apart from Ayurveda and Allopathy medicine Homeopathy also established its strong presence in Malabar. One significant matter regarding this area is that the first graduate Homeopathic Medical College in Asia was started in Calicut in 1796. This medical college is affiliated to Calicut University.

Paramedical courses are equally important like medical courses also. General nursing, BSc. nursing, B. Pharm and M. Pharm. are some of the essential paramedical courses in the state. The Malabar region had no enough facilities for these courses for several decades after independence. Earlier Calicut Medical College was the only institution in Malabar that offered paramedical courses. But when government realised the need of these courses they permitted self-financing institutions in the state. Al-Shifa College of Pharmacy, Devaki Amma College of Pharmacy and Jamia Salafiya College of Pharmacy, Grace College of Pharmacy (Palakkad), are the pharmacy colleges in Malappuram. National College of Pharmacy and JDT College of Pharmacy are the unaided pharmacy colleges in Kozhikode. Moulana Institute of Paramedical Sciences, (Perithalmanna), College of Paramedical Sciences (Perithalmanna), MIMS College of Allied Medical Sciences (Vazhayoor) are the other paramedical institutions in Malabar.

Al-Shifa Nursing College (Perithalmanna), Moulana College

of Nursing (Perithalmanna), MES College of Nursing (Perithalmanna) and EMS Memorial Co-operative Nursing College are some of the nursing colleges in Malappuram. BSc. Nursing is the course offering in Nursing Colleges. Increase in the demand for nurses inside and outside the country government permitted several unaided nursing schools to offer Gen. Nursing degree in Kerala. The lack of facilities for Nursing courses the students were forced to go to Karnataka and Tamil Nadu for the study. Nirmala College of Nursing, Baby Memorial College of Nursing, National Hospital College of Nursing, PVS College of Nursing and KMCT College of Nursing are some of the unaided Nursing Colleges in Kozhikode that meet the needs of the students of Malabar.

Once north Malabar region had no facilities for nursing courses and the students had to study nursing in other states. This situation underwent change with the beginning nursing courses by unaided nursing colleges in Kannur district. They provided 250 nursing seats for BSc. Nursing course. College of Nursing (Pariyaram), Koyili College of Nursing (Kannadiparamba), Canossa College of Nursing (Cherukunnu), College of Nursing (Anjarakady) and Lourde College of Nursing (Taliparamba) are the unaided nursing colleges in Kannur. Among the districts of Malabar, there are no nursing colleges in Wayanad and Kasargode districts. General Nursing is the course offering in the Nursing Schools. These schools are attached to the hospitals in all the districts of Kerala.

There was only one dental college in Malabar attached to Calicut Medical College. Recently government sanctioned self-financing Dental Colleges in Malabar. MES Dental College (Perinthalmanna), Educare Institute of Dental Sciences (Chattiparamba) and Malabar Dental College and Research Centre (Edappal), Royal Dental College (Palakkad), KMCT Dental College (Kozhikode) are the unaided dental colleges in Malabar.

Table 7.2 : The Increase of Professional Colleges and Seats in Kerala 2000-2008

Year	*Colleges*	*Seats*
Medical Colleges		
2000-2001	6	800
2007-2008	18	2100
Engineering Colleges		
2000-2001	23	6300
2007-2008	87	26430
Nursing Colleges		
2000-2001	1	50
2007-2008	77	3850

Source: Philip Njaralakkat, 'Self-Financing Professional Colleges in Kerala: Current Issues in the Limelight' in K. S. Mathew and T.K. Sebastian (ed.) *Indian Constitution, Education and Minorities in Kerala*, IRISH, Kannur, 2009, p. 345.

Legal Education

Malabar had no facilities for legal education till 1970. In the colonial period Malabar was under the jurisdiction of Madras High Court and many lawyers from Malabar worked in Madras. After independence they shifted to Kochi where the High Court of Kerala is situated. The students of Malabar gained their legal graduation from the law colleges of Mysore, Madras, Kochi and Thiruvananthapuram. The first law college of Malabar was started in Kozhikode in 1970[2]. Three year Bachelor of Laws (L.L.B.) was the first course started in this college and the first batch of lawyer passed out of the college in 1973. In view of heavy response from the part of students government upgraded this only college in Malabar to a postgraduate college by starting L.L.M. (Master of Law) in 1976 with the specialisation of Law of Taxation.

In 1982, the college was shifted to new separate buildings and they started five-year L.L.B. course in 1994. The students after passing S.S.L.C. joined for five-year L.L.B. after qualifying an entrance examination. All courses of the university are affiliated to Calicut University. As a part of special arrangement the college started evening course in L.L.B. for candidates who are employed in government service. Through this course the students can acquire an original degree like regular students of the college. Many officers who attained L.L.B. degree through evening batch enrolled as lawyers and became successful law practitioners after retirement from the government service.

Management Education

The new economic policies of the government like Liberalisation and Privatisation led to a great demand for people with managerial and information technology skills. Consequently, several colleges started offering BBA, BCA, MBA, MCA and Hotel Management courses in Kerala. Earlier there was only very limited facilities for the management education in Malabar. The School of Management Studies, a university department under Calicut university was the first institution in Malabar that offer management education in Malabar. But a landmark in the management education of Malabar was the starting of the prestigious Indian Institute of Management (IIM) in Calicut in 1996. Thuchath Ezhuthachan College of Management, Information Technology and Bio-Technology, Yuvakshetra Institute of Management Studies, Royal Institute of Science and Technology, Sreepathy Institute of Management and Technology (Palakkad), Farook Institute of Management (Kozhikode), SNES Institute of Management Studies and Research (Kozhikode) are the self-financing management institutions in Malabar.

Another section in Management education is degree courses in hotel management, hospitality and administration. Bachelor of Hotel Management (BHM) is a four-year course and has great scope for employment both inside and outside the country. Some colleges provide B.Sc. Hotel Management and Catering, B. Sc. Food Science and Quality Control,

Bachelor of Tourism and Hotel Management and so on. The students who passed these degree courses have been in great demand in tourism and hotel industry in the country. Oriental College of Hotel Management in Wayanad, Baitul Issa Arts and Science College, Kozhikode, I.C.N.A.S. Kozhikode, Yuvakshetra Institute of Management Studies are some of the unaided colleges in Malabar that offer some of the above mentioned degree course in hotel management. Govt. College, Koylandy (Kozhikode) and C.K.G. College, Perambra (Kozhikode) give B.Com. in Hotel and Tourism Management. Another popular course in this category is B.A. Travel and Tourism and Master of Tourism Adminstration (MTA). Pazhassi Raja College, Wayanad offer both of these courses in Malabar. Besides, Govinda Pai Memorial Govt. College, Manjeswaram, Don Bosco College, Wayanad and Providence Women's College, Kozhikode admit students for B.A. Travel and Tourism.

The government facilities failed to come forward to the needs of the society according to the recent trends in education. When several new courses started in other neighbouring states the governments in Kerala did not take any steps in this direction several years. In this case also private agencies invested huge amount of money for educational institutions providing medical, paramedical and management courses. Instead of supporting such unaided institutions government policies sometimes had created several hardships to the managements. If self-financing professional institutions were not established in Kerala it would be a great loss to the students.

References

1. To control the self-financing educational institutions in Kerala government passed two laws and some of the unconstitutional provisions of these acts were challenged by the managements in the court. These are The Kerala Self-financing Professional Colleges (Prohibition of Capitation Fees and Procedure of Admission and Fixation of Fees) Act 2004 and The Kerala Professional Colleges or Institutions (Prohibition of Capitation Fees Regulation of Admission, Fixation of Non-Exploitative Fee and other Measures to ensure Equity and Excellence in (Professional Education) Rules, 2006.

2. The classes of the law college were started in Government Training College building in Mananchira in Kozhikode. Professor. M. Krishnan Nair and Professor P. Ramakrishnan were the first principal and lecturer of the college respectively.

8

Conclusion

The development of education is the chief factor for the all round development of a country. In the growth of literacy Kerala one has been a model not only for India but also for other developing countries of the world. The literacy rate in the state in 1991 was 90.2 per cent vis-a-vis 52.1 per cent for the country. This achievement was not attained suddenly but its seeds were sown by the period of missionary activities in Kerala. The missionaries of London Missionary Society (LMS) and Church Missionary Society (CMS) established educational institutions in Travancore since the beginning of the nineteenth century and the same role was played by the Basel Evangelical Mission (BEM) in Malabar. The foundation laid by these missionary societies in Kerala was an important factor for the future educational development of Kerala. At the same time the diminutive institutions of colonial government failed to provide education to all castes of the society. But this lacuna was filled by the educational institutions started by the private institutions including the missionary societies.

The colonial government recognised the role of private institutions in educational development of the society. The most important indication of this recognition was the introduction of grant-in-aid system by the British government since 1854. Through the grant the government shared the burden of the private individuals in providing education to the common people in the society. The colonial authorities realised the fact that it is not possible to give elementary education to the children with the active participation of private agencies. They ensured the cooperation of the common people in sharing the expenses of education through 'Rate Schools'. The education of women and backward classes was more improved not in the government schools but in the schools under missionaries. As a factor of social change among the dominant caste in the society, the colonial government expressed special interest in the education of Mappilas of Malabar. The British recognised modern secular education as the best way to change the anti-British attitude of the rebellious Mappilas of Malabar. Consequently in the Mappila schools the colonial government encouraged secular education and grant-in-aid was also provided to these institutions.

In the educational development of Travancore and Kochi the role of native rulers was crucial. This interest was the part of the welfare measures introduced by the rulers. This support was absent in Malabar since it was under the direct rule of the British. During the colonial period and till the formation of Kerala state there was breakthrough in growth of education in Malabar. Moreover the attitude of the people of Malabar towards education was not favourable and infrastructure facilities were very poor especially in the rural areas. This situation began to change with the advent of migrant farmers to the highland of Malabar. As mentioned earlier these migrants had given utmost importance to the education of their children. A question raised among them was whether to start church or school first. They gave more importance to the education of their children and built buildings for school along with places of worship. In many places the church and school shared the same building and this was a new experience to the natives of Malabar because the local people were generally averse to available education. The migrants established more than 500 schools in rural areas of Malabar and it was landmark in the growth of education in Malabar. The poor farmers did not get any support from the government or other agencies for the beginning of this school. They collected all the resources including land, money, wood and labour for the construction of the schools. Usually 'School Committees' were formed in many places under parish priests for the construction of the school buildings. Securing recognition for the school from the government and bringing qualified teachers were some of the duties of this Committee. The farmers had showed great interest in donating land and wood to the construction of the schools. *Pidiyari, Ulpannapirivu, Bespukkanachitty* and so on were usual methods employed by the migrants for raising money for the construction of the schools. Besides, the migrants organised *Pothupani* for the speedy completion of manual work for the schools. The great dedication and unity expressed by the migrants in the beginning of schools highly improved the educational facilities of Malabar. But the government institutions lacked infrastructure, teachers and facilities at the same time that reduced the interest of the people in the public schools.

The higher education facilities in Malabar were very insufficient and the people generally showed little interest in higher education. The intervention of the colonial authorities in the improvement of the collegiate education was paltry. When the number of pupil who completed their school education increased the people began to show interest in the establishment of new colleges in Malabar. Apart from efforts of the missionaries, private agencies under Muslim and Christian sections took great interest in the beginning of new colleges. The establishment of Farrok College and St. Joseph's College in Calicut; and NSS college at Palakkad were the best instances of private intervention in the higher education of Malabar. The establishment of Calicut University and later Kannur University gave a great impetus to the advancement of higher education in Malabar. The migrants and many Christian congregations set up UG and PG colleges in the highland of Malappuram, Kannur, Kasargode and Wayanad. Moreover, community organisations like MES, SNDP and NSS were at a race in the beginning of colleges in different parts of Malabar in 1960s. The College Committees formed by local people especially Muslims resulted in the beginning of both aided and unaided colleges in this region. The few government colleges established in Malabar were not enough for the growing need of the society and the government was reluctant to start sufficient college because of the huge investment. In this situation parallel educational institutions began to cater the higher education needs of the students.

The scarcity of teacher training institutions in Malabar was a serious matter in the education sector of Malabar. The government neglected the establishment of such institutions in Malabar. When this handicap seriously affected the education sector of Malabar, the migrants under the leadership of Fr. George Kizhakkacahlil established a Teacher Training Institute in Wayanad in 1963 which was a turning point in the educational progress of the highlands of Malabar. But the government's apathy in the beginning of training institutes and colleges resulted great hardships to the students because they had to go to other countries, even Assam to have a B.Ed. Degree course. Till the middle of 1990's government did not allow private individuals in starting unaided training colleges in the state. To provide teacher education the universities established University Teacher Education Centres and it was great help to the students. But by 2000, government sanctioned large number of unaided B.Ed. Colleges in the state and Malabar also greatly benefited from it. In Malabar alone 34 unaided B.Ed. Colleges were started and it was enough to meet the needs of the students. Moreover, M.Ed. Courses were started in many colleges including in unaided centres and such higher qualifications have been improving the quality of teacher education in the state.

The government and people neglected technical education and training in Kerala for a very long time. The lack of skilled manpower had been considered an important reason for the industrial backwardness of Kerala. When the people of Kerala started large scale labour migration to Gulf countries in 1970's and 1980's, they felt several difficulties due to the lack of technical knowhow. The job seekers had only very limited facilities for diploma and degree courses in different branches of engineering. This situation was on account of government's reluctance to start enough polytechnics and engineering colleges in the state. Moreover, the government engineering colleges were not having enough training facilities and courses were out of date. The huge initial investment and financial burden incurring in new government and aided engineering colleges prevented the government from new colleges. This situation also changed when government started permitting unaided engineering colleges in the state since 2000. Large number of unaided engineering colleges were started by individuals, religious authorities, co-operative societies, government agencies and so on. The number of seats in the engineering colleges in the state increased to more than 30000 by 2007.

The demand for conventional courses among the new generation of students decreased in the new economic condition of the country. Due to economic progress and privatisation in economy the industries needed specially trained and highly qualified candidates. In the medical education sector there was only one Allopathic medical college in Malabar and it was not able to provide medical aid to even one-tenth of the people of Malabar. The seats for MBBS and MD were sufficient for the students of Malabar. This handicap was also overcome when the government sanctioned medical colleges in private and co-operative sector. Some dental colleges are also established in private sector in Malabar. Private Ayurvedic medical colleges were also sanctioned by the government in Malabar region. The lack of nurses and paramedical staff led the government to permit private nursing schools and colleges and allowed several new courses in the paramedical field.

The scope of management education in Kerala increased due to the need of managers in the private institutions inside and outside the country. For the BBA and MBA courses the students of Malabar had to rely on institutions outside the state, but in recent years government sanctioned self-financing management courses in many arts and science colleges. Moreover, separate institutes for management studies were also established in private sector. The growth of tourism sector all over Kerala led to the development of hotel industry in Kerala. Many institutes offering degree and diploma in hotel management were started in many parts of Malabar in private sector and students who passed these courses attained jobs outside the state and in foreign countries. The people of Malabar had special interest in computer education because of the availability of jobs due to recent boom in Information Technology sector in Bangalore and Madras. So, large number of self-financing engineering colleges and arts and science colleges started offering BCA and MCA courses in Malabar.

In the educational progress of Malabar the role of government was not satisfactory for three or four decades after independence. The students of Malabar either had to go to distant places or leave their aim of higher education due to the lack of higher education facilities. Earlier Kerala has been resisting the self-financing institutions on the ground of frivolous reasons. But at the same time the neighbouring states like Tamil Nadu and Karnataka had started large number of self-financing institutions and attracted students from Kerala. The recent policy change of the Kerala government in sanctioning self-financing institutions helped the educational progress of the country. The private agencies came forward abruptly to start large number of institutions. In short the private investment in the education sector of Kerala played most important role in the educational progress of Malabar.

Select Bibliography

Primary Sources

Kozhikode Regional Archives (Education Department)

Bundle No. 1

Serial No. 31, *Go. No. 354, 12/03/1921*

Serial No. 25, *Go. No. 326, 13/03/1922*

Serial No. 78, *Go. No. 497, 20/04/1922*

Serial No. 91, *Go. No.113, 26/01/1922*

Bundle No. 4

Serial No. 67, *Go. No.1987, 20/01/1926*

Serial No. 67, *Go. No.1987, 20/01/1926*

Serial No. 67, *Go. No.1987, 20/01/1926*

Government Publications and Reports

Academic Calendar 2009-10, Government College of Teacher Education (hereafter GCTE), Kozhikode, 2010.

Acquittance Roll of the Establishment of the Malabar Christian College, (School Department) March, 1923, Calicut.

Acquittance Roll of Teachers, B. E. M. Elementary School, Hosadurg, March, 1935.

Administration Report 1907-71: Collegiate Education, Ernakulam, 1973.

Administration Report of the Department of Collegiate Education 1987-88, Ernakulam, 1988.

Administration Report on Technical Education 1964-65: Kerala, Ernakulam, 1966.

Administrative Report 2005-2006, Nair Service Society, Chenganassery, 2006.

Admission Register 1951-56, Vol. 1, Government Training College, Kozhikode, 1951.

Anjukollathe Nettangal-Malabar District, Information and Publicity Department, Government of Madras, Madras, 1951.

Annual Report 1944-45, University of Travancore, Trivandrum, 1946.

Census of India 1981-Final Population Totals: Kerala, Trivandrum, 1982.

District Statistical Hand Book- Cannanore District, Department of Economics and Statistics (Hereafter DES), Trivandrum, 1981.

Economic Review 2007, State Planning Board, Govt. of Kerala, Thiruvananthapuram, 2007.

Educational Statistics 1987, Directorate of Public Instruction (hereafter DPI), Govt. of Kerala, Thiruvananthapuram, 1987.

Educational Statistics since Independence, DPI, Trivandrum, 2007.

Election Guide 2006, Malayala Manorama, Kottayam, 2006.

Examination Scheme 1929, Madras Secondary School Leaving Certificate, Government Press, Madras, 1929.

Fact Book on Manpower: Kerala 1988, DES, Thiruvananthapuram, 1988.

General Register of Admission and Withdrawals 1952-53, Government Vocational Higher Secondary School, Nadakkavu, Kozhikode, 1953.

Guide Book 1965-66, Department of Education (hereafter DE), Govt. of Kerala, 1966.

Guide Book 1988-89, DE, Govt. of Kerala, 1988.

Guide Book to the Teaching of English in Schools, DPI, Madras, 1952.

Indicators of Kerala Development 2007, DES, Thiruvananthapuram, 2007.

Kerala Educational Statistics 1972-73, DPI, 1973.

List of Recognised and Aided Elementary Schools in Central Malabar District 1952, Madras, 1953.

Madras Education Rules, Government Press, Madras, 1941.

Madras Education Rules, Government Press, Madras, 1950.

Man Power Series 61: Kerala, DES, Thiruvananthapuram, 1988.

March to Education in Kerala 1958, Publication division, Government of Kerala, 1974.

Register of Admission and Withdrawals 1950-54, Sarvajana High School, Sulthan Bathery, 1954.

Report of Survey on Unrecognised Schools in Kerala, DES, Thiruvananthapuram, 2007.

Report of the Survey on Parallel and Tutorial Colleges in Kerala 1989, DES, Thiruvananthapuram, 1990.

Report on Public Instruction in Madras Presidency 1917-18, Vol.1, Madras, 1919.

Selected Indicators of Development- Kerala and India, DES, Thiruvananthapuram, 1995.

Self Appraisal Report (Submitted to NAAC), GCTE, Kozhikode, 2008.

Sree Narayana Directory 2009 (Kerala Kaumadi), Thiruvananthapuram, 2009.

Statistical Hand Book of Kerala 1965, BES, Trivandrum, 1965.

Statistical Hand Book of Kerala 1970, BES, Trivandrum, 1971.

Statistics for Planning 2009, DES, Thiruvananthapuram, 2009.

The Fort St. George Gazette, Education Department, Madras, 1951.

The Fundamental Rules and Subsidiary Rules of Government of Madras, Government Press, Madras, 1945.

Secondary sources

Souvenirs

Aksharacheppu 2005, B.E.M. Girls Higher Secondary School, Kozhikode, 2005.

Aksharakerala, Saksharatha Smaranika, Kannur, 1991.

Centenary Souvenir 1892-1992, Visitation Congregation, Kottayam, 1992.

Darppanam, Souvenir of Education Committee, Sulthan Bathery Panchayat, Wayanad, 2009.

Devalaya Prathishta Smaranika, Infant Jesus Forane Church, Kanhangad, 2002.

Devalaya Prathishta Smaranika, St. George Church, Kanjiradukkam (Kasargode), 2005.

Devalaya Prathishta Smaranika, St. George Church, Paduppu (Kasargode), 2003.

Devalaya Prathishta Smaranika, St. Joseph Church, Panathadi (Kasargode), 2005.

Devalaya Prathishta Smaranika, St. Mary's Church, Panathur (Kasargode), 2006.

Devalaya Prathishta Smaranika, St. Thomas Church, Kolakkad, 1996.

Directory 2007, Archeparchy of Kottayam, Kottayam, 2001.

Directory, Diocese of Palghat, 2006.

Directory, The Syro-Malanakara Catholic Major Archiepiscopal Church, Sulthan Bathery, 2003.

District Human Development Report: Wayanad, Thiruvananthapuram, 2009.

Edavaka Directory 2008, St. Mary's Forane church, Maruthomkara, 2008.

Francion 09, St. Francis English Medium School, Thottada, Kannur, 2009.

Golden Jubilee souvenir 1949-1999, St. Sebastians's Church, Koodaranji,1999.

Golden Jubilee Souvenir, St. Joseph's Aided U. P. School, Chempanoda, 2003.

Golden Jubilee Souvenir 1955-2005, St. George Church, Vilangad, 2005.

Golden Jubilee Souvenir, Holy Family U. P. School, Padathukadavu, 1999.

Golden Jubilee Souvenir, St. Joseph's H.S.S., Kodenchery, 2005.

Golden Jubilee Souvenir, St. Thomas Forane Church, Udane, Shirandy (Karnataka), 2005.

Hand Book, Providence Women's College, Calicut, 2009.

Hrydayapurvam, Devalayapratishta Smaranika, St. Sebastian's Church, Manadukkam, 2005.

K.C.Y.M. Smaranika, Kannur, 1994.

Koodarajiyude Charitrathalukalil, Kallukulam Kudumbayogam, Chenganassery, 2006.

Kudiyetta Suvarna Jubilee Smaranika 1949-1999, Palavayal, 1999.

Magazine 1991-92, Pazhassi Raja N.S.S. College, Mattannur, 1992.

Malabar Knanaya Kudiyetta Suvrana Jubilee Souvenir, Kannur, 1993.

Millennium Magazine 1972-2001, Little Flower Girls High School, Kanhangad, 2001.

Navathi Smaranika: A Krishnan, Smaranika Committee, Chalode, 2003.

Nirmalagiri 1992, Nirmalagiri College Magazine, Kuttuparamba, 1992.

Orma, Kannur Mahotsavam, Kannur, 2005.

Padhadhi Rekha 1997-2002, Irikkur Block Panchayath, Irikkur, 1997.

Padhadhi Rekha 2002-2007, Kannur Jilla Panchayath, Kannur, 2002.

Padhadhi Rekha 2004-2005, Kannur Jilla Panchayath, Kannur, 2004.

Padhadhi Rekha 2005-2006, Kannur Jilla Panchayath, Kannur, 2005.

Padhathi Rekha 2002-2007, Kasargode Jilla Panchayath, 2002.

Padhathi Rekha 2008-09, Kanhangad Nagarasabha, Kasargode, 2008.

Padhathi Rekha 2008-2009, Kasargode Nagarasabha, 2008.

Paithrukam, Golden Jubilee Souvenir, St. Mary's Church, Udayagiri, 2007.

Paurohitya Rajatha Jubilee Smaranika, Rev. Fr. Thomas Thythottam, Iritty, 1989.

Platinum Jubilee Smaranika, St. Joseph's Forane Church, Vayattuparambu, 2007.

Poornima, The Quinquennial Souvenir, Msgr. Raymond Memorial School, Chembanoda, 2007.

Pouravakasa Rekha, Kasargode Jilla Panchayath, Kasargode, 2009.

Rajatha Jubilee Smaranika 1978-2003, Thalassery Athirupatha Madyavarjana Prasthanam, Thalassery, 2003.

Rajatha Jubilee Smaranika, Bishop Vallopilly Jubilee Memorial High School, Perumpilavu, 2007.

Rajatha Jubilee Smaranika, Nazareth Sisters, Kunnoth, 2000.

Rajatha Jubilee Smaranika, Santhome Higher Secondary School, Kolakkad, 2007.

Rajatha Jubilee Smaranika, St. Joseph's High School, Kunnoth, 2008.

Rajatha Jubilee Smaranika, St. Mary's Church, Urippukutti, 2007.

Rajatha Jubilee Smaranika, St. Mary's High School, Maruthomkara, 1982.

Rajatha Jubilee Smaranika, St. Sebastian's Church, Padichira, 1998.

Rajatha Jubilee Smaranika, St. Thomas High School, Manikkadavu, 2001.

Retirement Souvenir, St. Mary's High School, Pariyapuram, Malappuram, 1998.

Saksharatha Smaranika, Kanichar Panchayath, Kannur,1991.

School Pravarthana Report 2007-08, U. B. M. S. L. P. School, Hosadurg, 2008.

Seb's Voice, St. Sebastians Higher Secondary School, Koodaranji, 2001.

Shabdam: Mahath Janmashadabdi Smaranika, Diocese of Kannur, Kannur, 2005.

Silver Jubilee Smaranika, Prabhath Arts Club, Maloor, 1992.

Silver Jubilee Souvenir 1977-2002, Society of Kristudasis, Mananthavady, 2002.

Silver Jubilee Souvenir, St. Mary's Church, Kariyappilly, 2007.

Silver Jubilee Souvenir, Durga High School, Kanhangad, 1973.

Silver Jubilee Souvenir, St. George High School, Kulathuvayal, 1980.

Silver Jubilee Souvenir, St. Mary's High School, Maruthomkara, 1983.

Souvenir, St. Joseph's U. P. School, Kunnoth, 2005.

Spandanam, St. Joseph Church, Varakkad, 2007.

Suhrutham, Devalaya Smaranika, Holy Family Church, Nellipara, 2009.

Suvarna Jubilee Smaranika 1954-2004, St. Sebastian's Church, Velimanam, 2004.

Suvarna Jubilee Smaranika 1957-2007, St. Thomas U. P. School, Karikkottakari, 2007.

Suvarna Jubilee Smaranika 1995-2005, St. Mary's Forane Church, Alakkode, 2005.

Suvarna Jubilee Smaranika, N. R. Pura Migration, N.R. Pura, 2002.

Suvarna Jubilee Smaranika, St. Georgre Church, Puravayal, 2007.

Suvarna Jubilee Smaranika, St. Thomas Church, Kunnoth, 1992.

Suvarna Jubilee Smaranika, St. Mary's Church, Kilianthara, 1999.

Suvarna Jubilee Souvenir 1951-2001, St. Mary's Forane Church, Cherupuzha, 2001.

Suvarna Jubilee Souvenir 1957-2007, St. Joseph's Minor Seminary, Thalassery, 2007.

Suvarna Samvatsarangal, Fathima Matha Church, Kudiyamala, 2003.

Uparipadanam, Mathrubhoomi Directory, Kozhikode, 2006.

Varshikakoshavum Yathrayayappum, U. B. M. S. L. P. School, Hosadurg, 2008.

Vidyalaya Pathrika 2004-05, Kendriya Vidyalaya, Kasargode, 2005.

Vista 2009, Rani Jai Higher Secondary School, Nirmalagiri, 2009.

Yobel 1956-2006, St. Joseph's College, Devagiri, Kozhikode, 2006.

Journals

Advances in Arts and Ideas

Endeavours in Education

Indian Economic and Social History Review

Indian Educational Review

Indian Journal of Teacher Education (*Anweshika*, NCTE)

Journal Educational Planning and Administration

Journal of the Institute for Research in Social Sciences and Humanities

Journal of Education for Sustainable Development

Journal of Indian Education

Journal of Research and Extension in Education

Journal of Studies in Teacher Education

Journal of Value Education

Studies in History

Newspapers

Girideepam

Malayala Manorama

Mathrubhoomi

Mangalam

Deepika

Personal Interviews

A. C. Varkey, President, Farmers Relief Forum, Nadavayal, 13-02-10.

A. E. Damodaran, Ezhava migrant Thodupuzha, Nadavayal, 20-12-10.

A. E. Poulose, Appilliyil, Malankara, Sulthan Bathery, 22-11-10.

A. P. Kunjananthan Nair, Chazhivayal, Muttil, 10-03-10.

A. V. Chacko, Migrant from Aryannur, Nadavayal, 13-02-10.

A. V. Kalan, Uralikuruman, Padikunnu Colony, Nadavayal, 15-04-10.

Abdul Sattar, PTA President, Iqbal HSS, Kanhangad, 28-03-2010.

Aboobakkar, Muslim Migrant from Ottapalam, Erulam, 27-12-10.

Abraham, Mullanpottakkal, Orthodox Church, Malankarakunnu, 18-09-10.

B. K. Gurumallappa, Padiri, Pulpally, 05-04-10.

B. S. Jinesh, Tharakan caste, Mananthavady, 12-03-10.

Bhaskaran Puramadathil, migrant farmer, Kolery, 11-05-10.

C. A. Kunjiraman Nair, Eachome, Kaniyambetta, 12-06-10.

C. J. Varkey, Chamakkalayil, migrant farmer, Kaniyaram, 24-04-10.

C. K. Janu, President, *Adhivasi Gothara Mahasabha*, 16-11-10.

C. N. Sankarankutty, former Deputy Tahasildar, Ambalavayal, 22-07-10.

Cheriyakullan, Kattunaikan tribe, Alumula colony, Puthadi, 02-09-10.

Chonkan, Adiya tribe, Aryannur colony, Panamaram, 16-10-10.

E. J. Joseph, Member, School Committee Kudiyanmala, Kannur, 19-02-2010.

E. M. Thomas, Edathanal, migrant farmer, Chennalode, 23-04-10.

E. Prabhakaran Nambiar, Puthadi, 27-01-10.

E. Ramankutty, Kunduvadiyan tribe, Erulam, 22-12-10.

Fr. Paul David, Manager, Corporate Schools of CSI, Calicut, 29-07-2010.

G. T. Venkitaraman, Telungu Brahmin, Mananthavady, 12-03-10.

J. P. Raghavaih, Research Scholar, Calicut, 05-09-2010.

John Xavier, Uppuveetil, Poomala, Sulthan Bathery, 05-04-10.

Jose Thomas, Thekkanat, migrant farmer, Mullankolly, 20-07-2010.

K. C. Narayanan, Rtd. Head Master, Pulpally, 01-03-2010.

K. K. Reghunathan Nair, former teacher, Durgha HSS, Kanhangad, 26-03-2010.

K. K. Sreedharan, former Principal, S. A. L. P. School, Thariyode, 25-09-2009.

K. Keshava Patteri, Senior Clerk, HS, Nileeshwaram, 28-03-2010.

K. M. Kunjabdullah, Teacher T.R.K. HSS, Pangode, 13-06-2009.

K. R. Balan, Head Master, Sarvajana High School, S. Bathery, 08-05-2009.

K. R. Balan, HM, Sarvajana High School, S. Bathery, 08-05-2009.

K. Sadanandan, Rtd. Teacher, Malabar Christian HSS, Calicut, 19-082009.

K. Shivarajan, former Director, UTEC, Calicut, 03-03-2010.

K. Thamban Nair, Former HM, Durga HSS, Kanhangad, 26-03-2010.

K. U. Mathai, former President, Pulpally Panchayath, 21-10-2009.

K.K. Naha, Owner, Single Teacher School, Parappanagadi, 08-09-2009.

N. K. Vijayan, Assistant Director, DTE, Kasargode, 15-01-2009.

P. A. Parameshwaran, Rtd. A.E.O Wayanad. Mananthavady , 23-10-2009.

P. E. Shambu Namboodiri, Raja's HS, Nileeshwaram, 28-03-2010.

P. K. Reji, Principal, CKRTTI, Pulpally, 27-11-2009.

P. Kelu, former HOD of Education, Calicut University, 07-12-2009.

P. Lakshmanan, Director, UTEC, Calicut, 09-02-2009.

P. O. Sreedharan, Rtd. Teacher, SKMJ HSS, Kalpetta, 09-11-2009.

P. Radhakrishnan, President, Parallel College Association, Kannur, 07-10-2009.

P.D. Babu, Assistant Registrar, Kannur University, 10-05-2010.

P.K.M. Tarakan, Vice-Chancellor, Kannur University, 11-05-2010.

P.S. Hymavathy, Teacher, Govt. HSS, Nadakkavu, 16-07-2010.

Sherija Beatrice, HM, BEM UP School, Calicut, 28-12-2009.

Sreekrishnan Agathiyar, HM, Govt. HSS, Hosdurg, 27-03-2010.

Sushila Chittyagam, Rtd. Teacher, BEM UP School, Calicut, 07-03-2009.

T. Mohan Babu, Director, MBTC, S. Bathery, 20-04-2009.

Thomas Joseph, Nellikunnel, former head master, Nadavayal, 15-04-2010.

Thomas Philip, HM, St. Mary's High School, Maruthomkara, 16-03-2010.

Thomas Thekkanat, President, School Committee, Mullanakolly, 23-09-2009.

Books

Alexander, P. J. (Ed.), *Higher Education in Kerala*, Trivandrum, 1983.

Ali, K. T. Muhammad, 'Development of Western Education among the Mappilas of Malabar' in *Journal of Kerala Studies* (hereafter *JKS*), 14,1-4 (1987).

Bai M., Meera, *Technical Education in Kerala: Emerging Trends*, New Delhi, 2009.

Dilip, T. R., *School Educational Attainment in Kerala: Trends and Differentials*, CDS Working Paper Series 429, Thiruvananthapuram, 2010.

Ennolam: Vidhyalaya Charitram-Kozhikode (Mal.), DDE, Kozhikode, 2004.

Ghosh, Suresh Chandra, *The History of Education in Modern India*, Orient Longman, New Delhi, 2009.

Jose, C., *Kudiyettacharitravum Thamarassery Meghalayum* (Mal.), Thiruvampady, 1998.

Joseph Kuravilangad, *Konippadikal* (Mal.), Kozhikode, 1991.

Joseph, K. V. *Migration and Economic Development of Kerala.* New Delhi, 1988.

Kathleen Gough, 'Literacy in Kerala' in Jack Goody (ed.) *Literacy in Traditional Societies,* Cambridge, 1975, pp. 133-160.

Kumar, C. E. Ajith, and Lathika M., 'Revisiting Kerala's Performance on the Education Front', in *Review of Development and Change*, 12.2 (2007) pp. 169-189.

Kumar, Ratheesh and Parthasarathy, D., 'Global Interventions in Educational Reform- DPEP and the New Curriculum: The Case of Wayanad District in Kerala', in *Journal of Educational Planning and Administration* 21,4 (2007) pp. 353-370.

Kurup, K.K.N., *Adhunika Keralam: Charitra Gaveshana Prabhandagal* (Mal.), Thiruvananthapuram, 1995.

Kurup, K. K. N., 'Significance of the Studies Based on the Archival Collections in the Mission House in Basel with Special Reference to Kerala', in *JKS*, 5, 3-4 (1978), pp. 457-461.

Kutty, E. K. Ahamed, 'Islam and Social Reform Movements in Kerala' in *JKS*, 5, 3 and 4 (1978), pp. 439-456.

Kutty, E. K. Muhammad, The Development of Arabic Education in Kerala: A Survey, in *JKS*, 9,1-4 (1982) 453-464.

M. Vijayakumari Amma, 'A Historical Perspective on the Teacher Education Programme in Kerala', in *JKS*, 33, 1 (2005), pp. 219-252.

Mangamma, J., *The Rate Schools of Godavari*, Government of Andhra Pradesh, 1973.

Mariadas Kuzhippil, *C.M.I. Sabhayude Malabar Kudiyettam* (Mal.), Cochin, 2001.

Mathew, A., *Christian Missions Education and Nationalism*, Delhi, 1988.

Mathew, K. S. and Sebastian, T. K., *Indian Constitution, Education and Minorities in Kerala*, Tellicherry, 2009.

Menon, A. Sreedhara, *A Survey of Kerala History*, Kottayam, 1996.

Mettleda, T., 'Government-Management Relation in Education 1817 to 1957', in *JKS*, Trivandrum, 7, 1-4, (1980) 342-350.

Muhammad, U., *Educational Empowerment of Kerala Muslims: A Socio-Historical Perspective*, Calicut, 2000.

Nair, K. N. and P. R. Gopinathan Nair, *Higher Education in Kerala: Micro Level Perspective*, New Delhi, 2008.

Nair, P. R. Gopinathan and D. Ajith, *Parallel Colleges in Kerala: A Case Study of their Structure in Terms of Enrollment Costs and Employment*, Centre for Development Studies Working Paper No. 156 (hereafter CDSWP), Trivandrum, 1983.

Nair, P. R. Gopinathan, 'Education and Socio-economic Change in Kerala 1793-1947', *Social Scientist* 4, 8, (1976) pp. 28-43.

Pillai, P.P., *Kerala Economy: Four Decades of Development*, Aranattukara (Trissur), 1994.

Raghavan, J. Veera, (ed.) *Higher Education in the Eighties: Opportunities and Objectives*, New Delhi, 1985.

Ramkumar, Vasantha and R. Ramkumar, 'Development of Education in Kerala': 1960-71, in *JKS*, 15, 2 (1993), pp. 441-453.

Ramkumar, Vasantha and Ramkumar, R., Development of Education in Kerala: 1960-1971, in *JKS*, 12, 4-5 (1978), pp. 441-453.

Raza, Moonis, *Higher Education in India: Retrospect and Prospect*, Association of India Universities, New Delhi, 1991.

Salim, A. Abdul and Nair, P. R. Gopinath, *Educational Development in India*, New Delhi, 2002.

Sebastian,T.K., 'Educational and Occupational Mobility among the Migrant Cultivators of Malabar', *Journal of the Institute for Research in Social Sciences and Humanities* 2, 2 (2007).

Sreekala, P. S., *Keralathile Vidhyabhyasam Pachathalavum Parivarthanavum*, Thiruvananthapuram, 2009.

Tarakan, P. K. Michael, *Socio-economic Factors in Educational Development: The Case of 19th Century Travancore*, CDSWP No. 190, Trivandrum, 1984.

Thomas, Joseph A., 'Dynamics of Educational Development: A case study of Selected 'Backward' Villages in Kerala' in Vaidyanathan, A. and Nair, P.R. Gopinathan (Ed.), *Elementary Education in Rural India: A Grassroots View*, New Delhi, 2001.

Thomas, Joseph A., *Education and Economic Development*, New Delhi, 1998.

Varghese, N. V. and Sajeev, K. S., *A Study of Primary Schools in Kasargode District- Kerala,* NIEPA, New Delhi, 1997.

Varghese, N. V. and Sajeev, K. S., *Provisions and Performance: A Study of Primary Schools in Malappuram- Kerala,* NIEPA, New Delhi, 1997.

Varghese, N. V., Sajeev, K. S and Bijulal, M. V., *How Much Do Children Learn in Primary Schools? A Study of Wayanad District-Kerala*, NIEPA, New Delhi, 1998.

Ummerkutty, A. N. P., Affiliation System: A Study of Kerala Experience, The Kerala State Higher Education Council, Thiruvananthapuram, 2011.

Index

F

G

U

V

W

Z